THE ARTISTIC CRAFTS SERIES
OF TECHNICAL HANDBOOKS
EDITED BY W. R. LETHABY

SILVERWORK AND JEWELLERY

THE FOUNDRESS' CUP: CHRIST'S COLLEGE, CAMBRIDGE.

"*An Art can only be learned in the workshop of those who are winning their bread by it.*"

—SAMUEL BUTLER ("Erewhon").

"*One may do whate'er one likes
In Art : the only thing is to make sure
That one does like it—which takes pains to know.*"

—ROBERT BROWNING ("Pippa Passes").

A New Revised and Enlarged Edition, with special chapters, fully illustrated, based on demonstrations by Professor Unno Bisei and Professor T. Kobayashi of the Imperial Fine Art College at Tokyo, giving the traditional methods of Casting, Damascening, Incrustation, Inlaying, Engraving, and Metal Colouring still practised in Japan, with further chapters on Niello, on the making of Boxes and Card Cases, and a chapter on Egyptian and Oriental methods of work.

Plates originally printed in collotype are now reproduced in half-tone.

SILVERWORK AND JEWELLERY

A TEXT-BOOK FOR STUDENTS
AND WORKERS IN METAL
BY H. WILSON. WITH DIAGRAMS
BY THE AUTHOR
AND OTHER ILLUSTRATIONS.
SECOND EDITION, WITH NEW
SECTIONS DONE IN COLLABO-
RATION WITH PROFESSOR
UNNO BISEI OF THE IMPERIAL
FINE ART COLLEGE, TOKYO

NEW YORK   CHICAGO
PITMAN PUBLISHING CORPORATION

"*It is evident that the value of methods and apparatus so simple as these is dependent on the skill and talent of the worker who uses them. The hand of man, more perfect than any mechanism, is everywhere seen in early goldsmiths' work. When, however, mechanical methods develop, their exactitude, their even precision, their unintelligence, replace little by little that fascination which belongs to everything shaped by the human hand. One need not, therefore, be surprised that there is so much difficulty in the goldsmith's art, no less than in other branches of industry, in procuring things to-day which have the charm of ancient work. Mechanism has destroyed the habit of intelligent personal effort on the part of the worker, and his energies are now directed to the imitation of the cold and arid regularity of the machine.*"—"On Medieval Gold and Silver Work" ("VIOLLET LE DUC," vol. ii., p. 172).

PITMAN PUBLISHING CORPORATION
2 WEST 45TH STREET, NEW YORK
205 WEST MONROE STREET, CHICAGO

ASSOCIATED COMPANIES
SIR ISAAC PITMAN & SONS, LTD.
PITMAN HOUSE, PARKER STREET, KINGSWAY, LONDON, W.C.2
THE PITMAN PRESS, BATH
PITMAN HOUSE, LITTLE COLLINS STREET, MELBOURNE
27 BECKETTS BUILDINGS, PRESIDENT STREET, JOHANNESBURG
SIR ISAAC PITMAN & SONS (CANADA), LTD.
(INCORPORATING THE COMMERCIAL TEXT BOOK COMPANY)
PITMAN HOUSE, 381–383 CHURCH STREET, TORONTO

MADE IN GREAT BRITAIN AT THE PITMAN PRESS, BATH
D8—(D.5278)

EDITOR'S PREFACE

In issuing these volumes of a series of Handbooks on the Artistic Crafts, it will be well to state what are our general aims.

In the first place, we wish to provide trustworthy text-books of workshop practice, from the points of view of experts who have critically examined the methods current in the shops, and putting aside vain survivals, are prepared to say what is good workmanship, and to set up a standard of quality in the crafts which are more especially associated with design. Secondly, in doing this, we hope to treat design itself as an essential part of good workmanship. During the last century most of the arts, save painting and sculpture of an academic kind, were little considered, and there was a tendency to look on "design" as a mere matter of *appearance*. Such "ornamentation" as there was was usually obtained by following in a mechanical way a drawing provided by an artist who often knew little of the technical processes involved in production. With the critical attention given to the crafts by Ruskin and Morris, it came to be seen that it was impossible to detach design from craft in this way, and that, in the widest sense, true design is an inseparable element of good quality, involving as it does the selection of good and suitable material, contrivance for special purpose, expert workmanship, proper finish, and so on, far more than mere ornament, and indeed, that ornamentation itself was rather an exuberance of fine workmanship than a matter of merely abstract lines. Workmanship when separated by too wide a gulf from fresh thought—that is, from design—inevitably decays, and, on the other hand, ornamentation, divorced from workmanship, is necessarily unreal, and quickly falls into affectation. Proper ornamentation may be defined as a language addressed to the eye; it is pleasant thought expressed in the speech of the tool.

In the third place, we would have this

series put artistic craftsmanship before
people as furnishing reasonable occupa-
tions for those who would gain a liveli-
hood. Although within the bounds of
academic art, the competition, of its kind,
is so acute that only a very few per cent.
can fairly hope to succeed as painters and
sculptors; yet, as artistic craftsmen, there
is every probability that nearly every
one who would pass through a sufficient
period of apprenticeship to workmanship and design would reach a measure
of success.

In the blending of handwork and
thought in such arts as we propose to
deal with, happy careers may be found
as far removed from the dreary routine
of hack labour as from the terrible un-
certainty of academic art. It is desirable
in every way that men of good education
should be brought back into the produc-
tive crafts : there are more than enough
of us "in the city," and it is probable
that more consideration will be given in
this century than in the last to Design
and Workmanship.

. . . . . .

Work in the precious metals, the sub-

ject which is dealt with in the present
volume, seems especially to have suffered
from the slavish methods introduced, perhaps, to compete with machinery, and
from the general benumbing of the apti-
tude for design which affected so many
of the artistic crafts during the course
of the last century. On the other hand,
there have been signs of a danger that
these crafts may be victimised by glaring
affectations in design and by unashamed
crudeness of manipulation. Of the two
vulgarities—that of commercial dulness,
and that of the blandishments which
assume the name of "new art"—the
latter is likely to be by far the worse. On
this question of design it is essential to
guard oneself from a merely capricious
originality, a striving for exaggerated ele-
gance, and an endeavour to suggest ideas
of luxury, which last is probably the most
enervating and repulsive characteristic of
certain forms of modern taste.

Symptoms of these faults are often
found in a preference for violent curva-
ture of form, an introduction of unrelated
splashes of enamel, and the over-insistence
upon tool marks and chemically treated surfaces. On the contrary, we should rather

aim at reasonableness, at the natural development of traditional forms, and at pleasant, unobtrusive finish. The true method of design is always growth, not rootless egoism.

Of old the arts developed under the hand by the contact of tools and material. Now, for instance, it is far too customary to "design," as it is called, the shape of some vessel, be it for silver, or glass, or potter's clay, and then to coerce the material into the preconceived form. But any one who has watched the process of throwing a pot on the wheel, of blowing glass, or of beating up metal out of the sheet, will have noticed how dozens of vitally beautiful forms are produced on the way to the final dulness predestined by the drawing. The best complement to workshop practice is to study the old work stored in our museums, without intention to copy specific types, but to gather ideas generally applicable. From this point of view all ancient art is a vast encyclopædia of methods and experience.

The London student should frequent the Gold Room and Mediæval Department of the British Museum, the general

collection at South Kensington, and the
marvels of the Indian Museum. He
should also study the devices on ancient
coins, medals, and seals. It will be found
that such systematic study will not only result in the accumulation of hints for trade
purposes, but will be a true form of self-
culture; for all history stands as a background to these objects bequeathed to
us by past civilisations; and the perfect
knowledge of one thing includes the partial
knowledge of many things.

It is not for me to praise these books,
but I may be allowed to say that, in both
those now issued we have been given the
best knowledge of expert craftsmen, who,
having explored the past of the arts with
which they deal, have been willing to give
out the combined results of their experiments and study clearly and without
reserve.

W. R. LETHABY.

November 1902.

AUTHOR'S PREFACE TO FIRST EDITION

THIS book does not deal with the history of the jeweller's art. It is intended as a practical guide to some of the more simple processes of the craft. The worst fault of such a text-book, intended in the first place for students, would be vagueness. I have attempted to avoid this by describing the operations of each process consecutively from beginning to end.

This of necessity causes a certain amount of repetition, but anything is better than doubt. For the sake of clearness the various chapters have been written round the diagrams inserted in the text. These in most cases have been drawn from work actually carried out. It is not, however, my intention to impose conceptions of design upon the student, but only to describe methods I have found to give the best results in my own workshop. These methods, with such changes as the common sense of the worker will suggest, may be applied to

xiii

objects of whatever form carried out in
the same materials.

No student worthy of the name would
attempt to copy the designs for himself.
Not only is deliberate copyism dishonest,
it checks the development of the student's
native powers and stunts his individuality.
And while nothing is more pitiable than
a too conscious cultivation of our poor
little personality, whatever is felt to lessen
our power of work in any direction must
be studiously avoided and whatever helps
us eagerly sought. If the student will
study methods, materials, and natural
forms, perfect his skill in handiwork,
feed his imagination on old work, attend
faithfully to his instincts, his personality
can safely be left to take care of itself.
It will infallibly find expression.

One most valuable stimulus to the
imagination is to be found in the descriptions of marvellous metal work by old
writers, poets, historians, and travellers.
The old inventories of church plate,
though they do little more than catalogue
the objects, yet will often give most suggestive hints for design. What could be
finer than this from the inventory of the
jewels and relics belonging to the cathedral
church of Sarum, made by Master Thomas

Robertson, treasurer of the same church, in the year 1536 :—

" Item, a cross with Abraham offering up Isaac, and a lamb behind him with an angel (wanting one wing), and on the left side the images of Abel and Cain, weighing 63 ounces and a quarter."

One sees the thing through the old scribe's eyes, and straightway the mind begins to work on a scheme of its own.

Another valuable aid is that given by old descriptions of methods and processes. The treatise of Theophilus, published by Murray, contains many hints. The translator, however, not being a craftsman, missed many points in his rendering, and the technical descriptions are not as clear as could be wished. I have endeavoured to rectify this defect in the new renderings given at the end of this book ; but Hendrie's Theophilus will always be full of interest to those curious in the arts of the Middle Ages.

It is, of course, impossible in a limited space to treat of a limitless art ; moreover, many processes, such as wet and dry colouring of gold, die-stamping, gold-lapping, frosting, and electro-plating and typing have too little connection with art to be considered at all. I hope, however, that the processes described in this book may help the student to acquire a technique for himself. If it does anything, however slight, in that direction its object will have been achieved.

H. W.

AUTHOR'S PREFACE TO SECOND EDITION

THE demand for a new edition gives a welcome opportunity of correcting the many errors of omission and commission in the first edition.

It has also made possible the addition of chapters on Raising, Box-making, Engraving, and Niello.

The chapter on Raising has been added to supplement that in the first edition which was based upon the directions given by Theophilus in the *Book of Divers Arts*. The new chapter describes the more modern methods of raising, and although of necessity summary and incomplete, may perhaps suffice as an indication of the principles involved.

More important still, through the most beautiful generosity of Professor Unno Bisei of the Tokyo Fine Art College, who first initiated me into the mysteries of Japanese inlay, Damascene work, and Patinas, I am able to devote several sections to these important subjects. The chapters dealing with them are based on his instructions, supplemented by observations arising out of personal experience in the methods described.

Knowing as one does with what care craft processes are kept secret in this country, and with what jealousy all inquiry is checked, the utter selflessness and simplicity with which Professor Unno Bisei, one of the most remarkable craftsmen in the world, explained and demonstrated his methods, giving without stint the results of his inimitable skill and wide experience, was at once rebuke and inspiration.

I feel that it is impossible in any set phrase to thank him sufficiently for what he has done for myself and for my fellow workers in the craft.

My thanks are also due to Professor T. Kobayashi of Tokyo for the demonstration and recipes of Japanese methods of metal colouring given at my request before the students of the Royal College of Art. The methods and recipes whenever tried give beautiful results, although, since the personal equation counts for so much, the results may not always be those expected.

I have to thank Mr. C. Jagger for his notes and drawings of engraving tools, Mr. G. Jones for his illustration of some of the Japanese methods, and Messrs. Murphy and Wiseman for assistance in the chapter on Raising and Niello-work, and Mr. G. Cowell for his notes on the making of card cases, and to Mr. Sakujiro Semoto for his translation of Professor Unno Bisei's lecture.

I am indebted also to Mr. Kiralfy of the White City for permission to photograph the native craftsmen, and specially indebted to Mr. Gardiner, the superintendent of the Indian section, and Mr. Tulsei Ram Khuttri, Mr. Ardeshir, and to all the kindly helpful craftsmen who posed, explained and demonstrated the secrets of their craft with the sweet willingness of accomplished artists to whom nothing is secret, by whom nothing is withheld, and in whose souls the creative fire burns with unfading lustre.

H. W.

CONTENTS

xviii

CHAPTER VI

PAGE

CHAPTER VII

CHAPTER VIII

CHAPTER IX

CHAPTER X

CHAPTER XI

xxi

CHAPTER XXIV

CHAPTER XXV

CHAPTER XXVI

CHAPTER XXVII

CHAPTER XXVIII

CHAPTER XXIX

CHAPTER XXX

Contents

CHAPTER I

INTRODUCTION

The exquisite jewellery of Egypt, Etruria, and Greece, work so fine as almost to appear miraculous, was the outcome of centuries of development. What remains to us is the sum of an infinite series of small improvements in work and method, added by one generation of craftsmen after another. Each worker brought his fraction of beauty to the store laid up and bequeathed to him by those who had gone before. The men who made these things which fill us all with wonder had, however, not only inherited skill to guide their hands and eyes. Each went through a long apprenticeship, during which he was made free of the results of an unbroken tradition of craftsmanship.

His work lay almost in the open air; there was beauty in all his surroundings, and inspiration waited on him continually. As always the happiness of the worker was reflected in the work. Each seems to have been content if he could surpass by ever so little the skill of his forbears.

Yet the farther the discoveries of archæology take us back into the past, the more clearly we see by what slow, tentative, almost stumbling steps that perfection of skill has been attained. Between the prehistoric fibula hammered out from a nugget of ore and the granulated cloak-clasp of Etruria and Greece the distance is enormous, yet we are able to follow the line of development and almost to mark its stages. Apart from the fact that this gradual perfecting of craftsmanship has been the way to excellence in the past, it is the only way by which the student can attain to confidence and knowledge. Lacking these no one can give adequate expression to his ideas. Not only does the study of methods and the qualities of material enable the worker to give expression to an idea, it is absolutely the most fruitful source of ideas, and those which are suggested by process are invariably healthy and rational. The hand and the brain work together, and

26

the outcome of their partnership is a sanity of conception, which is greatly to seek in most even of the best work of to-day. The reason is perhaps that the zeal of the artist has not been tempered by know-ledge. The reason of this again is that for more than a century the painter and the sculptor have stood before the public as the sole representatives of the Arts, and in consequence all the crafts and arts have been approached pictorially, even by those who practise them, as if each were only another form of picture-making.

This is not wholly untrue, only the methods of the painter do not always apply in the crafts. Take as the simplest example a Rhodian ear-ring. What is it? —a rough pearl, a skeleton cube of gold wire, a tiny pyramid of beads, and a hook. What could be more simple? yet the cunning collocation of these ele-mentary forms has produced a thing of beauty that cannot now be surpassed. No amount of fumbling with a pencil could ever lead to a like result. The material was there in front of the crafts-man, and on the material the creative idea engendered the work of art. Art is craftsmanship plus inspiration; and

27

inspiration is the rush of unconscious
memory along channels made by a habit of
craftsmanship. But the craftsmanship of
the early workman was frank and fearless,
the worker of to-day is hidden behind the
stones he uses. His material is a screen
and not a medium of expression. Stones
and jewels to the early artist were means
of adding emphasis to his work, or were
used as the germ of a design; by the
modern they are used as substitutes for
design. To the former the jewel was an
added beauty to the setting; to the latter
the jewel is a means of hiding the setting
and the workmanship. The old workman
took the rough crystal of sapphire, or
ruby, or emerald, and polished it, keeping
the stone as large as possible, displaying
to the utmost its native beauty. The
modern workman splits and cuts his gems
into regular, many-faceted, geometrical
forms of infinite ingenuity and intolerable
hideousness.

The modern method of cutting equal-
ises the colour and intensifies the glitter
of the gem, but the glitter takes away
that mysterious magical quality, that inner
lustre of liquid light, which for the artist
is its chiefest beauty, and replaces that

28

beauty by a mechanical sheen offensive to every cultivated eye. Moreover, the machine-made perfection of the cut stone has, as it were, reacted on the mounting, and is, perhaps, one cause among many of the mechanical hardness and lack of artistry so visible in modern work. The student who is seeking to avoid these defects must begin at the beginning, learn thoroughly the rudiments of his craft, and build up his system of design by slow degrees out of the results of his daily experience. He must learn to rely at first on excellence of handiwork as the foundation of his claim to be considered an artist. The one guiding principle of all true craftsmanship is this: the forms used in design should express naturally and simply the properties of the particular material employed.

CHAPTER II

Materials—Educational Value of Process—Composition of Pickle—Pitch for Repoussé Work.

THE student will probably find that it is better at first to buy his silver plate already rolled to the thickness required, and have the wire drawn by the dealer; but later on he will find that he can draw small quantities of wire with a draw-plate fixed in a vice, and with a little care and practice he can thin out small ingots of metal on a stake or small anvil to any required thickness. He will in this way get a knowledge of materials quite impossible of attainment under any other conditions. The old craftsmen took full advantage of the native qualities of their materials, and these can only be learned by daily practice in working them. In the process of work ideas are matured which would otherwise have lain dormant and useless. The design gradually acquires those indefinable qualities of naturalness, simplicity, and sincerity which are found to a supreme degree in almost all old work.

The copper used should be of the best quality procurable. French or Swedish copper, such as is used for enamelling, is the best. For cloison wire, alloy copper, which is very nearly pure, should be used. Electrotype copper, which is very pure, can be used to alloy silver and gold.

For tools the finest tool steel in round,

30

square, or flat bars should be used. A
few pounds of block tin will be useful
for making moulds, and for use as a
block on which to stamp up with punches
small beads, discs, and leaves. It is less
yielding than lead for this purpose and
gives a cleaner result. It can also be
used as a backing for work in thin sheet
silver or gold. Much Etruscan work was
backed in this way. The impressed ornaments on mediæval chalices were often
filled and attached to the body of the work
by tin used both as solder and filling.

A block of zinc, weighing about 3 lbs.,
will also be useful for making moulds
in which sheet metal can be roughly
beaten up to shape ready for chasing.

Brass wire of different sizes is useful
for making temporary pins for joints,
and, if of good quality, can be used in
making silver solder.

Binding-wire of several gauges, ranging
from 18 to the finest, will also be wanted for
tying work together while being soldered.

Borax should be bought in crystals.
A small piece of slate on which to grind
it up can be got anywhere, or you can buy
a borax dish made of stone ware.

A small quantity of sulphuric acid, hydrochloric acid, and nitric acid will be wanted for the various pickling solutions. They should be obtained from a wholesale chemist.

Nitric acid pickle = 1 part nitric acid and 6 parts water.

Sulphuric pickle = 1 part acid and 6 parts water.

Hydrochloric pickle = 1 part acid and 8 parts water.

A pound or two of best boxwood sawdust will be wanted and kept in an ordinary biscuit box. It is used for drying the work after washing. The drying can be hastened by putting the box on an iron plate supported over a spirit-lamp or gas flame. The sawdust must not be allowed to burn or the work will be stained and the stain is rather difficult to remove.

Pitch for repoussé work is best made as follows :—

Pitch	.	.	.	4 parts.
Rosin	.	.	.	4 ,,
Plaster of Paris		.	2 ,,

Melt the pitch and rosin together in a pipkin, and when both have been well mixed and stirred, put in a small knob of tallow or an inch or two of tallow candle and again stir the mixture. Now add the plaster by handfuls and stir it in well. Then pour it out into a box well whitened with dry whitening, and leave it to cool. For winter work the pitch may be found too hard. It can be softened by remelting and adding another piece of tallow candle to the mixture.

Some boxwood sticks, $\frac{1}{4}$ inch square, for polishing, will be very useful.

A horn mallet is almost necessary for raising work, while a few different sized stakes to fix in the vice for hammer work are quite indispensable; very good ones can be made out of poker heads or the handles of fire-tongs.

CHAPTER III

Tools.

THE tools most likely to be required are:
For Repoussé work—

Chasing hammers (fig. 6), two sizes, one heavy and one light.

c

Various punches or chasing tools (fig. 7). An assortment of these, from forty to fifty, will probably suffice for most simple work.

Except for very special purposes, such as damascening and inlay work, or for touching up cast work, avoid the use of matting tools, or tools intended to produce a patterned or granulated surface. It is far better to rely on modelling and design for producing variety of surface.

A set of doming punches for doming the metal, and a small doming-block.

A set of files—round, flat, and three-square—and a set of needle files.

A pair of slide pliers.

A set of ordinary scorpers.

A set of engraving scorpers.

A few draw-plates. These can often be purchased second-hand.

Snarling-irons. These you can make for yourself out of lengths of bar steel.

A small cold chisel.

A bench vice. Those which revolve on a pivot are the most useful for general purposes.

A joint tool for making hinges.

Two or three pliers—round-nosed, flat, and ordinary.

34

Two pairs of cutting shears, one straight and one curved.

A jeweller's frame saw and fine piercing saws.

A square bench stake, which can be of steel. The bottom of a flat iron will do almost equally well for this.

A few slips of boxwood for making punches and for light mallets will be found very useful.

A drill stock, which should be one of the ordinary Swiss centrifugal drills. The drills for this can either be bought or made as the student desires.

A sand-bag, a pitch-block with a leather collar to keep the work in its place, and a blow-pipe and some form of spirit-lamp with a good large flame, will complete the list of students' requirements.

The student should make as many tools as possible for himself. This is particularly the case with drills, repoussé tools, and dies and punches of all kinds. In fact, there is very little indeed that the student cannot make for himself. Apart from the valuable experience to be gained in this way, a tool that is made for a particular purpose is almost always

35

better than one that is bought; while
the pleasure of having made it for oneself more than compensates for the
trouble.

CHAPTER IV

Work Benches—Best form of Bench—The Pin—
The Skin—Tool Rack—Board Sweep.

THE best bench for the worker is "the
French or jeweller's bench" which consists (fig. 2) of a hard beech board with
a semicircular hole cut out of the front
to receive the body of the worker when
seated. In the centre of this bow, a
small wedge-shaped piece of wood called
"the pin" is inserted to form a rest
for the work when filing or engraving.
The bench should stand very firmly
and be fixed to the floor, so that there
is no spring in the board when struck
with the hammer. Underneath the
board, around the bow of the semicircle,
a leather sheepskin is nailed to form
a receptacle for the filings of gold and
silver and to hold the tools while working. Many jewellers prefer tin trays to
catch the filings, but the latter have this

disadvantage, that work dropped from the bench is more likely to be injured

Fig. 1.

on the tray than if it fell into the skin. On the right-hand side of the bow the

37

flame for the blow‑pipe should be ar‑
ranged (see fig. 1, which shows a bench
arranged for five workers). If gas be used
the ordinary bench blow‑pipe is fixed

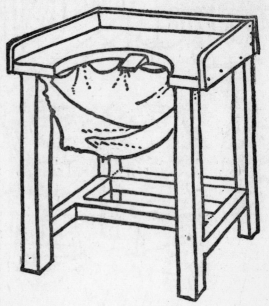

FIG. 2.

sufficiently near to the edge to enable
the flame to be directed towards the
centre of the semicircular space. If a

38

lamp be used it would naturally be placed in the same relative position.

There should be a rack at the side of the bench for tools, arranged so that the tools can be reached with the least possible loss of time and temper. Fixed on the floor underneath the bench you may have a movable grating of wood to catch any stray filings, and to prevent those which fall from being trodden into the floor and lost. The bench and the floor underneath must be swept every day and the sweepings preserved. When a sufficient quantity has been gathered, the sweep should be burnt in an iron tray to remove any trace of organic matter, the resulting ash well tried over with a magnet to remove any bits of iron wire, and the sweep sent to the refiners, who, after making an assay, will allow for the precious metal it may contain.

CHAPTER V

Wire-Drawing—The Draw-Bench—Draw-Plate—
Tube-Drawing—How to make a Draw-Plate.

WIRE is made by drawing short rods of metal either by hand or by means of a

39

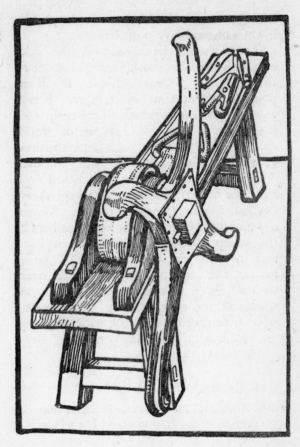

FIG. 3.

draw-bench (fig. 3) through the successively diminishing holes in a draw-plate (fig. 4). If the rods are small in section and the quantity of wire required is also small, the draw-plate can be fixed in a bench vice and the rods drawn through by hand.

To do this, first hammer the end of the rod taper so that it will come through the hole nearest in size to the diameter of the rod. This taper tip must be strong enough — when it has come through — to stand the pull of a hand-vice. Rub the rod with beeswax and draw it through the plate; the rod will be found thinner and longer. Do this with the next hole, and the next, until you have drawn it down to the required size, taking care to anneal it frequently as each drawing naturally hardens and compresses the sub-stance of the rod. If the wire

FIG. 4.

has to be very much reduced in size, or if there is a large quantity to do, it will be better to use a draw-bench, but the principle of the operation is the same in both cases.

Small tubes can also be drawn in this
way out of strips of sheet metal. Cut a
strip of metal of the length and thickness
you require, and the breadth roughly thrice
the intended diameter of the tube; cut the
end taper and with a hammer form it into
a sort of gutter lengthwise; anneal it and
oil it or rub it over with a little beeswax
inside and out and put the taper tip
through the wide end of the hole which
most nearly fits; insert the tip of a pointed
burnisher under the hollow of the trough
of the metal and into the back of the hole
(fig. 5), then draw the metal through the
hole. The burnisher helps to keep the
metal true as it folds round it while being
drawn through the hole. The rough tube
which results from this operation is annealed and drawn through the next smaller
hole, and so on until the desired size is
attained.

The student will find this very useful
in the preparation of tubing required for
hinges of brooches, lockets, boxes, and
caskets. If the tube is not large in
diameter all the work can be done in the
vice and without a draw-bench.

Hollow tubes of any section can be
drawn by using draw-plates with holes of

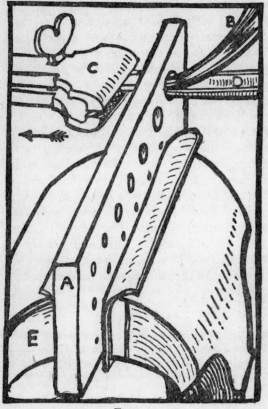

FIG. 5.

make his own draw-plate out of an old

flat file, first softening it, then punching
graduated holes with a taper punch of the
required section filed up out of bar steel
and properly hardened. The taper must
be very slight or the edge of the hole will
be too sharp, and will strip the metal instead of compressing it.

There are very few things necessary in
the workshop which a student cannot make
for himself. The curse of modern workshops is the dependence of the workman on
machine-made things. Rather than melt
an ingot and roll a small piece of metal for
himself to the exact size he needs, he cuts
a strip from a sheet in stock which is
nearest to the size. The effect on the
work is deplorable. The chief beauty—
the quality given by human handiwork—
is absent, and nothing can make up for
the loss.

CHAPTER VI

Repoussé Work—Chasing—Method of Procedure—
How to hold the Tools—The Behaviour of Metal
—Work in the Round—The Chasing of Castings.

REPOUSSÉ work is modelling in relief
produced by working with hammer (fig. 6)
and punches (fig. 7) on the back of a sheet

44

of metal fixed on some yielding material. Repoussé Work*
Chasing is work on the face of the sheet.
The term is also used for finishing up the
surface of castings. The required relief

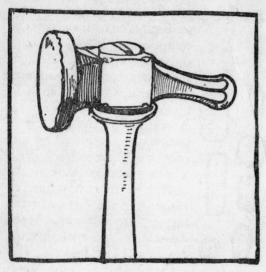

FIG. 6.

may be obtained either by beating down
the ground of the ornament, or by punching out the back and afterwards finishing
on the face.

If the relief required is very slight,
it may be obtained by laying the sheet

of metal on a block of lead, a piece of soft pine, or on a piece of thick cork matting. For higher relief the metal must be laid on a composition of pitch made as already described. The tallow makes the composition more yielding, and more will be required in the winter than in the summer. The metal is warmed and laid upon the pitch-block (fig. 8). A tracing of the pattern is secured to the metal by bits of wax at the corners. With a fine-pointed punch the outline is delicately pricked through to the surface of the metal. Or, if the work is too delicate to admit of this, the design may be transferred with carbon paper. This done, take rounded punches and beat down the ground of the ornament according to your intention. Get the relief gradually, let the blows be even in force, guide the punches so that the resulting furrow

FIG. 7.

46

makes a continuous surface and follows the form you may desire to express. At frequent intervals warm the metal on the surface, remove it from the pitch, and anneal it by making it red hot. This makes the metal yield more freely

Fig. 8.

to the blows of the punch. If this precaution is neglected the work will crack. By removing the metal from the pitch an opportunity is given of correcting any error from the front or back as the case may be. Punches with sharp edges

47

must be avoided until the last stages,
or the metal will tear. A few shaped
as in fig. 9 will be found very useful
for modelling the surface The student
should practise until the trace of the punch
on the metal is smooth and even from
beginning to end, and the lines from the
tracer clear and unbroken. Unless this

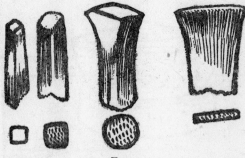

FIG. 9.

is done much time will be spent in correcting defects which might have been
avoided. Endeavour from the first to
acquire the right method of handling the
hammer and holding the punch. Any
chaser will show this in a moment. In
case none is at hand the appended diagram
(fig. 10) will make it clear. The punch
is held between the thumb and the first

48

and second fingers; the top of the third
finger rests on the metal as a pivot and
guide. A little practice will make this
action, at first difficult, afterwards almost
unconscious.

Fig. 10.

In high-relief work the relief is produced by alternately working on the back
and front; driving the ground down from
the front and the form out from the
back. With care, patience, and many
annealings, work may be done almost
in the round. For this work punches,
shaped somewhat like the tip of the

D   49

thumb, are most useful for getting the relief from the back, and rounded faced punches for the work on the front. These must be made by the student himself. In all repoussé work the main thing is to realise that metal is plastic, and with care can be led into forms or spread over surfaces like so much hard wax. This is especially true of copper, fine silver, fine and sovereign gold. Brass, even the best, is much less tractable. The student should be ever alert to seize the suggestions of decorative treatment of the metal which constantly arise while his work is in progress. The behaviour of the metal is more instructive than any teacher. Avoid the use of matted or grained surfaces except in cast work.

Work in the Round.—Small objects—birds, animals, little figures—may be done in repoussé by making the bodies in two halves. Solder the two together, in the way described farther on, leaving a small hole in the back or where it will least be seen. Fill the inside with pitch. This must be done by putting in small pieces and warming the object over the lamp. It may be found, however, that the pitch boils over and therefore that the object

50

will not be filled up properly. You must
then take soft pitch and with a metal
spatula or the flat end of a chasing tool
press the pitch into the hollow, warming
the metal from time to time.

Castings are chased as follows. The
rough projections and the pour which is
left where the metal ran into the mould
are first sawn off, the marks of the seams
are removed by small chisels, the object is
then warmed and fixed to the pitch-block,
and the surface modelled over with matting punches. Vents and other defects
in the casting are remedied by soldering
pieces of solid metal to make good the
deficiency. Holes are drilled out cleanly,
and pegs of metal screwed in, filed down,
and chased to the required surface.

CHAPTER VII

TAKE a sheet of metal, size 14 if the
cup is to be small to 16 if the cup

51

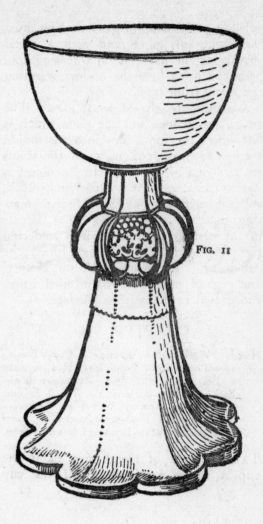

Hammer
Work

Fig. 11

is fairly large. Cut out a circle the diameter of which is a little larger than the contour of the cup. Take the compasses and lightly scratch on one side of the sheet a series of concentric circles, the smallest about an inch in diameter, increasing the radius of the succeeding circles by $\frac{1}{4}$ inches. These circles are to guide the hammer strokes. Now take a round-headed boxwood mallet

FIG. 12.

and beat the metal into a rough cup shape by beating it into a cup-shaped hollow in a wooden beating-block. This rough cup or shallow bowl must now be hammered into shape with a hammer shaped as in fig. 12 on a stake shaped as in fig. 13. Then begin on the inside and with the round-faced hammer, and keeping the elbow close to the side, beat

53

round in circles, using the hammer from
the wrist and not from the elbow. Repeat this, taking care to keep the blows
in concentric circles and to work regularly until the metal begins to take shape
and to feel springy. Then anneal it,
and, still using the same stake, beat on
the outside from the innermost circle outwards, taking care to leave the thickness

FIG. 13.

of the brim untouched. It may happen
that the cup has become uneven in shape;
this can be remedied after heating by
beating it out again from the inside, with
the box mallet, into the cup-shaped depression on the beating-block. Care must
be taken not to stretch the metal unduly
while doing this.

The work is then continued and is

almost wholly done from the outside, still keeping the blows in circles, turning the cup round with the left hand. A skilful hammerman at this stage, by regulating the inclination of the hammer face, can drive the metal in any direction, thickening the rim or the bottom or the sides of the cup as may be necessary. After the shaping of the cup is completed, it must be planished by using a hammer with a polished face, on a stake also polished for this purpose. When carefully done this leaves the surface true and bright and covered all over with brilliant facets. This method produces a cup beaten out of one piece. The form can naturally be varied at will, but it will often be found that the shapes taken by the cup during the progress of the work are much more interesting than those we set out to do. These suggestions of form should always be noted and worked out, either when the work in hand is done or frankly adopted as they arise.

The beaker form (fig. 15) is produced by the use of different stakes (fig. 14) or the beck-iron. Cut out your metal to the required size, making the diameter of the circle equal to the whole

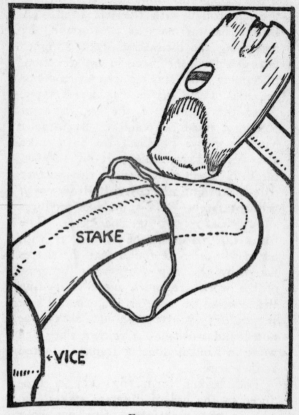

STAKE

←VICE

FIG. 14.

length of the profile line you propose

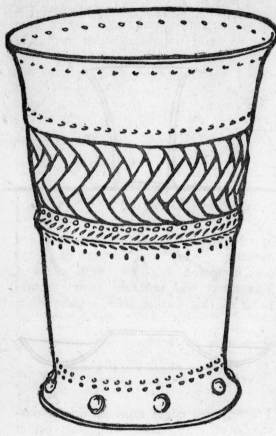

Fig. 15.

(fig. 15A). Make a central circle the size
of the base of the beaker and place the
tip of the curved stake against this line;
on this drive the metal away from you

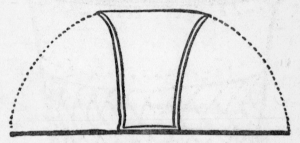

FIG. 15A.

by regular strokes of the rounded edged
hammer. Keep the circles of blows
concentric and the blows even in force.
The metal will probably assume something of this section after a short time.

FIG. 16.

The recurved edges must be driven outwards on the stake with the mallet
(fig. 14) and the work of the hammer

58

resumed until the general shape has been
attained. It can now be planished as
before described. The body of the
beaker or cup may be decorated with
raised surfaces (fig. 15), produced from
the inside by using snarling-irons (fig.
17). These are cranked punches Z-
shaped with ends of different form; one

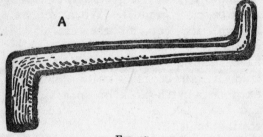

A

FIG. 17.

arm of the Z is fixed in the vice, the
other adjusted beneath the part of the
cup which is to be raised.

The Use of the Snarling-Iron.—The cup
is held in position with the left hand, and
the long arm of the snarling-iron struck
smartly with the hammer at A. This
causes the point of the snarler to strike
against the inner side of the cup with
nearly the same force as the original
blow. This method is employed where-

ever it is impossible, owing to the depth
of the cup or bowl, to use the hammer
or a tracing tool, and with care almost
any amount of relief can be obtained.
But as the metal is not supported by
pitch, which not only deadens the force
of the blow but holds the metal up
against the blow, much less force must
be employed, and the operation of raising
must be more gradual. When you have
brought the cup, by the use of the
hammer, to the shape you require, and
have planished it and made its shape
true, it can be filled with pitch and
fixed on a pitch-block or on a sand-bag
and completed from the face with
chasing tools.

Ornamentation. — Whatever ornament
you require must be such as expresses or
emphasises the forms of the cup. Spiral
lines or flutes or ribs, or combinations
of these, may be made to produce the
most delightful variations of surface.
Lozenges, zigzags, chevrons, any one
of these absolutely elementary forms,
repeated rhythmically on the surface,
will produce the pleasantest effect. You
must not set them out too exactly—trust
rather to eye and hand ; the variation

from geometric accuracy reveals the human worker, and it is the trace of the human touch which makes the meanest material precious. A cup with a narrow wreath of strictly formalised leaves and flowers bordered above and below by a good broad band of plain surface, and then enriched below, where the hand grasps it, with a chequer or continuous patterning of chevrons done by traced lines from the outside, will look dignified, rich, and workmanlike. Or you may raise a row of largish bosses with the snarling-iron and trace concentric lines round them and powder the surface with small bosses, mere punch marks done from the inside, and encircled from the outside; or you may, with a crescent-shaped punch cut for the purpose make rings of petals round one of these punch marks as a centre—always using as suggestion the effects produced naturally by the tools you employ.

If it be desired to add a base to the beaker, you will take a circle of metal as much greater in radius than the bottom of the cup as you wish the projection of the moulding to be. You will then dome it up in the hollowed wood-block

61

to get the rough shape, afterwards finishing it with hammers on the stake you used for the cup. Or you may put the dome on pitch and shape it with repoussé punches, taking care to avoid too much elaboration. The simplest rounds, chamfers, and hollows, with good broad surfaces to catch the light and reflections when polished, are always best. The student must not forget that these suggestions of design are only those which have arisen in my own experience. They are not to be taken as the only possible means of decoration. If the worker has any imagination — few are really without it, for imagination is only active love of beauty whether in Nature or in Art—then he will find the way for himself, his spirit and its manifestation in his work will be shaped to the thing he loves. A man's work is the mirror of his mind.

The joint between the base and the cup may now be made. The flat centre of the base must be cut away with the saw, leaving a broad fillet all round. Let each be well pickled in diluted sulphuric acid, scrape the joins well on the base and on the cup, paint both with borax

and water, tie the two together with
clips of strong binding-wire so that they
cannot slip about, and charge the joint
with paillons of solder dipped in borax,
and solder with the large blow-pipe and
foot-bellows, taking care to support the cup
so that it does not get bent out of shape
when hot. (See chapter xi. on Soldering.)

It will now be necessary to replanish
the cup on the stake, as the heat will have
taken all the stiffness out of the metal.
Any refinement of outline can now be
given, any roughness about the joint
filed clean, and the base made true on
the face-plate or upon a piece of plate-
glass. The same must be done for the
rim. The cup should be pickled again
until quite white and frosted looking.
It must next be stoned with a piece of
Water of Ayr stone to take away the
outer film of oxide. Unless this is done
you cannot get any proper polish or
show the real colour of the metal.

There is yet another method of making
a beaker. It is much easier but less
workmanlike. Turn up a conical tube
of metal and solder the joint carefully,
then hammer it out on the beck-iron
to any curve you please, always keeping

63

the hammer blows in concentric horizontal rings round the cup; make the
base as before, next solder to the base
a ring of plain, half-round, or twisted
wire the exact size of the bottom of
the body of the cup. This steadies the
body on the base and makes it easier
to tie the two together for the final
soldering. The cup can be planished,
filed true, and polished as before. Instead of planishing you may prefer to add
bands of zigzags or waves or mouldings
or a wreath of leaves. If so, fill the cup
with melted pitch, taking care to smear
the inside with oil or with whitening and
water beforehand, and let it cool. Warm
the pitch on the block, press the cup
mouth downwards on the melted surface and put a weight on the top until
cool, or, what is simpler, you can lay
it on a sand-bag and do without the
pitch-block.[1] The first method is however the most secure. Then sketch on
the ornament and outline it with a tracer,

[1] Work can be held on a sand-bag by a strap of stout
leather, one end of which is fixed to the bench, the other
end with a loop on it passes over the object, and through a
second hole in the bench. The foot is placed in the loop,
and the work held firm by pressure.

64

the ornament and outline it with a tracer, lightly if you do not want the lines to show inside and firmly if you do.

If, for example, you wish to raise a rounded band around the cup near the brim. Trace a line above and below all round the cup, the distance apart being the width of the moulding. You

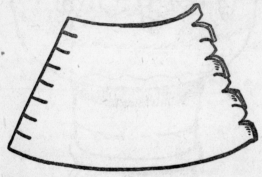

Fig. 18.

will then remove the cup from the pitch-block, warm it slightly in the blow-pipe flame, and take out the pitch. Then re-warm the pitch on the block, lay the cup on its side, and press it well into the pitch. The space between the two traced lines can then be beaten out with rounded punches to the projection

E

required. Other projections which may
be required lower down within the cup
must be done with the snarling-iron,

FIG. 19.

but these should only be very slight,
as the cup would be difficult to clean

when in use. Then clean, polish, and finish as before.

Another kind of joint which may be used in metal jugs or vases, or in any case where the joint does not matter, is the interlocking joint (see fig. 18). Cut out the metal to the shape required, making it ½ inch longer than is necessary for a butt joint, giving thus a lap of ¼ inch, and divide each of the edges to be joined into an equal number of spaces not more than ½ inch nor less than ¼ inch; cut these with the shears a little more than ¼ inch inwards and scrape both sides clean. Bend the alternate lappets of metal up and down on each half, fit the two together and solder firmly, flushing the joints thoroughly. The resulting tube or cone can now be hammered into shape and planished almost as if it were in one piece.

FIG. 20.

67

Fig. 19 shows a cup on a pillar-like base. The cup would be made separately as above described, and the base would be made as if it were a beaker. The raised mouldings on the stem (fig. 20) would be done with the snarling-iron and chased up from the front. The grapes and mouldings on the cup would all be done from the inside. The cup and base would then be soldered together as before. In the bottom of the cup you might place a small panel of the vine (fig. 21). Seen through wine a little ornament in a silver cup looks as if done in fine enamel.

FIG. 21.

CHAPTER VIII

Candlesticks—The Socket—The Shaft—The Scorer
—The Knop—The Base—Fitting Together—
Polishing—A Simpler Form of Candlestick.

Candlesticks FIRST take a disc of silver or copper, 10 gauge, 3 inches in diameter, beat it into

68

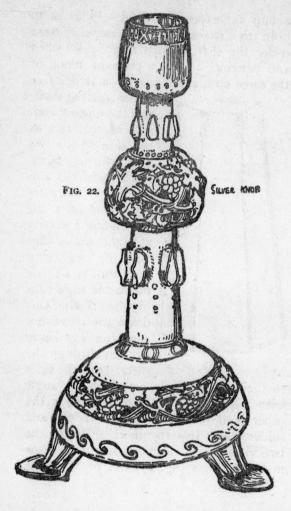

FIG. 22.   SILVER KNOP

a cup as before described. This is to hold the socket of the candle. Next make the shaft, which may be six-sided and tapering. Take a piece of metal of the same size, and draw upon it one face

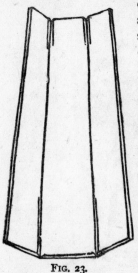

FIG. 23.

of the tapering shaft, and then, using each side of this face as one side of the two neighbouring faces, mark them out also (fig. 23) with a cutter made out of a file by bending the tang at right angles (fig. 24), the end being sharpened to a chisel point, the edge running lengthwise. Cut down the two inner angles until you have cut half through the metal, bend the sides to their proper angle, and flush the angle with silver solder. Repeat this for the other half of the shaft, and tie and solder the halves together. File up the two visible joins clean and smooth. Now make the boss (fig. 27) out of 10 gauge

70

by making a cup, and then drawing the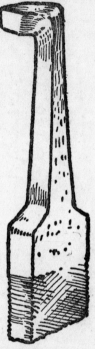
mouth gradually over on the curved stake
with the hammer shown
in fig. 25.

Planish it carefully, and
anneal it afterwards. Boss
out with a snarling-iron
a few shallow circular
bosses around the knop.
Now fill the knop with
pitch, and draw on the
circular bosses whatever
ornament you please.
You might, for example,
conventionalise the sym-
bols of the constellations
nearest the North Star.
Now make the guard-
dish with a circular raising in the centre, to form
a base for the shaft; beat
it up like a flat saucer,
planish it, and beat round
the edges other circular
panels, on which you will
place whatever you wish,

FIG. 24.

i.e. symbols of the seven planets as being
congruous with the first suggestion. Now
make two circles of twisted square wire,

71

one circle being right, the other left-hand twist, one circle just fitting outside, the other just fitting inside the rim of the guard-dish, and solder them to this edge (fig. 26).

On the circular raising you will solder a six-sided bearing-plate, and just within the edges of this bearing-plate you will solder a line of strong square twist. The space enclosed must exactly fit the base

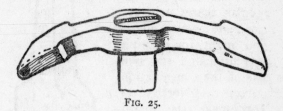

FIG. 25.

of the shaft, which will be strengtnened by a band of thick metal, surmounted by a ring of twist, and just above the bottom edge a second row of reverse twist arranged to fit exactly over the twist soldered on the plate on the guard-dish. To make the base, take a piece of No. 12, and beat it up into a cup with a flat bottom and tapering, slightly hollow sides. The rim of this cup will of course be the bottom, and the edge should have a broad flat beading

72

raised round it to strengthen it. You may
now arrange a few sprays of flowers round
this base, and after bossing them out from
the back, fill the base with pitch and chase
them up from the front. The socket for
the candle is a simple cylinder of No. 8,
long enough to project at least $\frac{1}{2}$ inch
above the edge of the smaller cup, and
having two rings of twisted wire soldered
round the upper edge.

You have now to fit the whole together.
First cut a hole in the knop (see fig. 27)

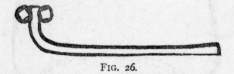

FIG. 26.

large enough to let the hexagonal shaft
through to the proper height (see fig. 25);
file the edges true, and then dome up a shallow cup of 14 metal to cover the bottom
of the knop. Cut a similar hexagonal hole
in this, and when it fits the shaft and the
knop properly, take them apart, and solder
the shallow cup to the knop. Next clean
the knop in pickle and slip it into place
on the shaft, and turn up a band of
metal about $\frac{1}{2}$ inch broad to fit the shaft

73

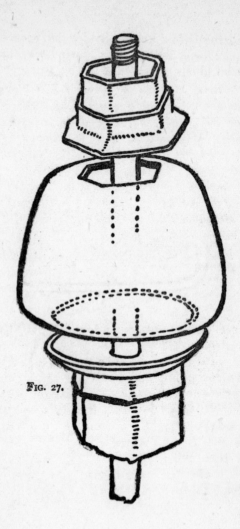

FIG. 27.

underneath the knop. Solder two rows of
square twist with a plain flatted wire between to the upper edge of this band. A
similar but smaller band having been fitted
to the upper part of the knop, the latter can
now be slipped into position and riveted
firmly there. You can now fasten this in
its place on the shaft with small screws
or rivets. Beat out a shallow cup out of
14 copper $\frac{1}{2}$ inch deep, and about 1 inch
outside diameter. Tap a screw on the
end of a piece of $\frac{1}{4}$-inch German silver wire
about 1 inch longer than the shaft, and on
the other end solder the shallow cup you
have just beaten out. You will now need
to cut plates of thick metal, size 14 or 16,
and after drilling a hole the size of the
centre rod, to fit them inside the top and
bottom of the shaft. These plates are to
prevent movement when the whole candlestick is screwed together. You will now
need a screw-nut and a washer-plate. Fit
all the parts carefully together, and screw
the nut tight. If there be any movement
it means that the bearing surfaces do not
fit each other, and the inequalities must
be filed away. When everything fits, the
whole can be polished with oil and pumice
and finished with rotten stone or crocus,

75

but do not remove the hammer marks. When it is all clean put it together finally, and darken the whole surface with a weak solution of sulphide of ammonium in hot water. Then wash it dry, and again polish slightly with a leather and a little rouge, and the work is complete.

Another form may be made thus :—

Beat up two deep funnel-shaped cups out of 14 copper, one larger than the other for the base, the smaller one for the top. When the shapes are true, make a shallow saucer-shaped cup a little larger than the top circle, and turn the edges over a stake with an edge to it, or over the edge of a hammer held in the vice. Then fit it on the top and carefully hammer the edge of the saucer down until it grips the edge of the cup. This makes the top of the candlestick. You will now need a boss to cover the meeting of the upper joint and lower portions of the candlestick. This is made either by beating up a deep cup as before described, then, after filling it with pitch, chase a wreath of olive or laurel or vine leaves, drawn carefully from nature, and arranged spirally round the boss beginning at the bottom.

76

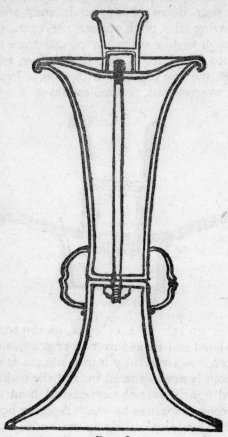

FIG. 28.

When you have got the relief, you can beat down the ground, and, after removing the pitch, pierce the openings through with a sharp tracer, and then fit it into its place, as described before, and fasten the two together with a central rod and a screw-nut. The candle-socket is

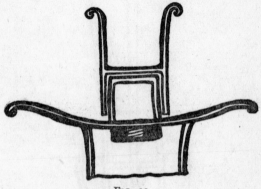

FIG. 29.

beaten up out of a cylinder, its top edge expanded and turned over (see fig. 29), and beaten down carefully into a rim; a false bottom is next soldered in, and the socket fitted lightly over the cylindrical head of the central shaft as before. Another boss may be made by beating up two cups; one, a little larger than the other, has its edges

78

spread out and turned over the lip of the
smaller bowl, as described for the top of
the candlestick. This makes a very simple
and sturdy-looking candlestick.

CHAPTER IX

Spoons—The Shape of the Bowl—The Stem—The
Handle or Thumbpiece—Joining the Bowl and
Handle—Second Method of Making a Spoon—
Third Method—Boxwood Punches—The Lead
Matrix—Ingots for Handles.

FIRST take a piece of silver, say 10 gauge, Spoons
mark on it the shape of the bowl (fig. 30)—
avoid the ugly modern shapes—and beat it
out with a boxwood mallet into a suitable
hollow in the beating-block. When you
have got it nearly into shape, true it up
on the rounded stake with a planishing
hammer. Then take a piece of $\frac{3}{16}$th
square wire or a strip of thick plate a
little longer than the handle you propose
and thicker, or you may cast a thick taper
ingot like a big nail. Then gradually
spread the top out wedge-shaped with
a hammer on the anvil, annealing the
metal from time to time. You may find
that as the metal extends it will crack at

79

Spoons

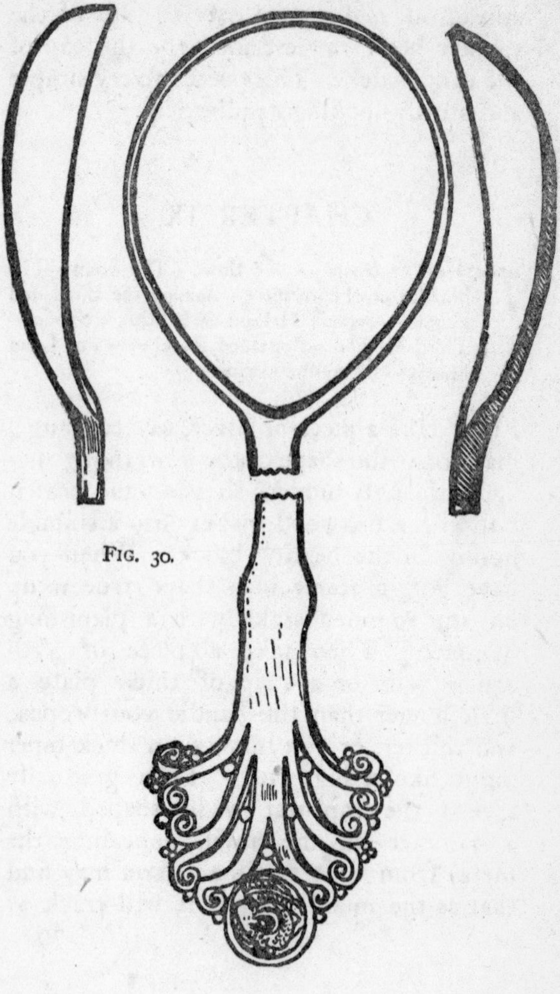

FIG. 30.

the edge, if so file away the crack with a triangular file; this prevents the crack from spreading. When you have spread it out a little more, take a chisel and divide the wedge into parts as shown in the diagram (fig. 31). Anneal it well, and bend the cut portions outwards (fig. 32), and hammer them carefully into long taper twigs. When you have done this neatly, anneal the metal again and coil

FIG. 31.

the twigs up as on fig. 30, or in any symmetrical way you may please. You will now solder the coils to each other, and further strengthen the joins by adding grains or groups of grains at the various points of junction. You will now have to fix the bowl and handle together. Hammer the end of the handle taper, leaving, however, a squarish projection at

F

81

the very end of the handle. This is to give a broader base for the attachment of the bowl. Unless the end of the

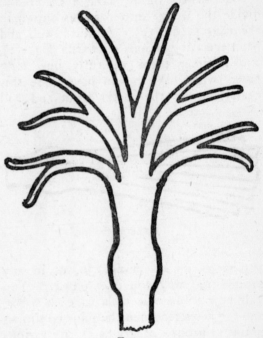

FIG. 32.

handle spreads out over the bowl where it joins, the strain put upon the spoon in polishing will soon tear the bowl and

82

handle apart. When you have tapered
the handle nicely, flatten out the square
projection fan-wise and
file it to fit the bowl.
Take a narrow strip of
iron about $\frac{1}{16}$th thick
and $\frac{3}{16}$th wide and tie
it firmly to the handle
with wire, so that the
iron projects beyond the
spoon end of the handle
by more than the length
of the bowl. You can
now tie the bowl and
handle together with
binding-wire and solder
the two together. This
done planish the bowl
upon a rounded stake,
both to harden the metal
and to correct any al-
teration in shape that
may have come about in
the soldering. Do the
same with the handle.
The work can now be

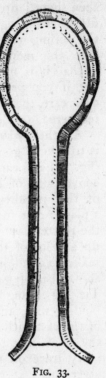

Fig. 33.

stoned and polished with pumice and oil,
finishing up with rouge.

Another way is to cast an ingot of the

83

rough shape of the bowl and shank together (see fig. 33). The whole spoon is
then shaped up with the hammer and the
file, after the ingot has been passed through
the rolling-mill once or twice to consolidate the metal. The objection to this
is that it is more wasteful of the metal,
but if you preserve the lemel with sufficient care, the waste can be almost entirely
recovered.

Another way of preparing the bowls
is to take a good-sized piece of boxwood
(fig. 34) and carve it into the shape of the
convex side of the bowl. An impression
of this is taken in modelling wax, and
a plaster-cast made from the wax. Trim
the plaster-cast into a square block, bend
up a piece of thin sheet metal so that it
makes an edging almost an inch high
above the top surface of the cast (fig. 35).
Tie this edging tightly round the cast with
binding-wire, and fill up round the edge
of the cast with a little thin plaster. Dry
the whole near the fire or in an oven until
every trace of moisture has disappeared.
Over this cast or mould, when it is perfectly dry, pour melted lead, and you will
have a mould of the concave side of the
spoon. Place this mould upon the anvil,

and a piece of 10-gauge silver on the Spoons
mould. With repeated blows on the boxwood punch drive the metal into the

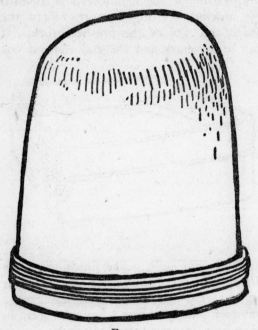

Fig. 34.

mould, annealing as often as may be
necessary. You will now have a rough
shape of the bowl; the superfluous metal
must be cut away, and the crinkled edges
85

hammered out smooth upon a rounded stake with a small tapping-hammer.

A good deal of hammer work in the preparation of the handle can be avoided by making the ingot more nearly the shape and size of the finished work. It can be flattened, and the end thinned out

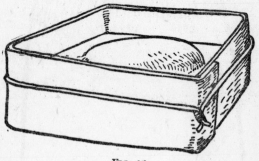

FIG. 35.

in the rolling-mill. The finishing can be done with the hammer on the stake as before. Do not be afraid of leaving the hammer marks where they are seen to have been necessary to produce the shape; they will always look beautiful. But the modern vice of putting in hammer marks to make a bad form look well, is more than reprehensible—it is foolish.

86

CHAPTER X

Silver Solder—Use of Scrap Silver—The Crucible—
The Ingot Mould—Enamelling Solder—Solders
for Large Work—How to Make Ingot Moulds.

IT is best always to make your own solder.
It will help to use up small scrap silver,

FIG. 36.

and is moreover cheaper to make than
to buy.

87

For ordinary work take two parts of silver cuttings and one part of fine brass cut small, and put them in a small fireclay crucible (fig. 36) with a little borax. Place the crucible carefully in the coke on the furnace, and put more coke round

FIG. 37.

it, leaving an opening in front and on the top. Then with the gas blow-pipe and foot-bellows direct the flame on the crucible, gradually increasing the force of the blast until the metal is fused. Care must be taken not to give more heat than

88

is absolutely necessary, or the zinc in the
brass will be oxidised, and the subsequent
fusibility of the solder impaired.

Have ready an ingot mould (fig. 37)
well greased; pour the fluid metal into
the mould, and leave to cool. When
cool you can roll it through the metal
rollers down to size 6 metal gauge, or
thinner if you want it for very small
work.

If fine brass cannot be obtained, fine
spelter or good pins will do equally well.

A very hard solder for use in enamelling
is made as follows :—

	oz.	dwt.	grs.
Fine silver .	1	0	0
Alloy copper .	0	5	0
	1	5	0

For a large piece of work requiring
many solderings the successive solderings
may be safely done by using a more fusible
solder for each operation.

The range of solder may be as follows :—

No. 1. 7 parts fine silver to 1 of fine brass.
,, 2. 5 ,, ,, ,, 1 ,, ,,
,, 3. 3 ,, ,, ,, 1 ,, ,,
,, 4. 2 ,, ,, ,, 1 ,, ,,

It is, however, rarely necessary to use so much precaution; care in the arrangement of the joints and in the regulation of the flame will make it possible to do with only one solder.

How to Make Ingot Moulds.—If you have not got an ingot mould one can easily be made. Take a piece of $\frac{1}{8}$th square iron wire, bend it up into the shape of a long U (fig. 38), file the edges true, and on one side of the U file cross nicks with a 3-square file. These nicks allow the air to escape when the metal is being poured in. Then take two

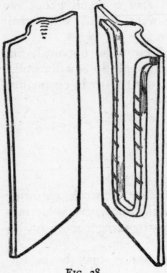

FIG. 38.

pieces of thick sheet iron a little larger than the U, and place one on each side of the U, and tie the whole together with binding-wire. Ingots of

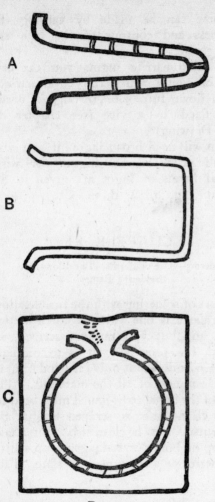

Silver
Solder

A

B

C

FIG. 39.

any size can be made by varying the
thickness and contour of the iron enclosing wire.

By using narrow ingots you can cast
slips of metal which can be afterwards
drawn down into wire through a draw-
plate fixed in a vice (see chapter on
Wire-Drawing).

You will need broad ingots if you wish
to roll plate, narrow ingots for wire.
Several forms of ingot are given in the
diagram (fig. 39, A, B, and C).

CHAPTER XI

Soldering—Use of Borax—The Blow-Pipe— Soldering Lamps.

THE art of soldering with the fusible alloys
given above is one which is much written
about and but very rarely described, although the process itself is exceedingly
simple. It demands only care and scrupu-
lous cleanliness of all the materials. The
parts of the metal to be joined must be absolutely clean—that is, scraped bright; the
solder itself must be clean also. First, take
a lump of borax crystal; grind up a little
with water on a small piece of slate. Take

92

a slip of solder, cut a number of slits
lengthwise down one end, and then, by a
few cross-cuts, snip off a number of tiny
bits or panels of solder. These panels
are then dipped in the borax, so that they
are completely covered by a thin coating
of borax. Next, the pieces of metal having been scraped clean along the join, are
both painted over with a solution of borax
by means of a camel's-hair brush. The
pieces are now to be tied together in their
proper positions by binding-wire. Care
must be taken here not to bring the edges
of the metal too closely together, or else
the solder when fused will run along the
angle instead of entering the joint. When
this happens the work looks as if it were
perfectly soldered, but on filing or putting
any strain on it the joint immediately falls
to pieces.

It is therefore important for silver
soldering that the work should be fitted
closely, but not too closely. Enough
space should be left for the metal to run
along the joint by capillary attraction.
When the two pieces of metal are fitted,
and bound together as described with iron
binding-wire, the joint is then moistened
with a brush charged with borax solution ;

93

the little chips of solder are then placed at intervals fairly closely along the joint. The work is then gently warmed in the flame of a blow-pipe to drive off the water in the borax. When this is dry a stronger

FIG. 40A.

flame is directed over the whole work, heating it gradually and evenly; take care that no part of the metal except that near the joins gets red hot. When the join has got thoroughly well heated, a

94

brisker flame may now be directed upon
the bits of solder. When using the blow-
pipe be very careful always to direct the
flame towards the worker and downwards,
so that he may readily see the heat he is

FIG. 40B.

giving and the heat the work requires.
If the work has been brought up to the
proper heat, the solder will immediately
flush and run along the joint, filling it in
every part. Wherever a portion of the
metal has been allowed to grow cooler

95

than the surrounding parts, the joint there will be imperfect, and the work must be cooled, the metal cleaned by being dipped into pickle—which is a mixture of one part hydrochloric acid and ten parts water; a stronger solution much used is half and half of each—and then the operation begun again until all the joints are full.

Soldering can be done either with the gas flame and mouth blow-pipe, with the

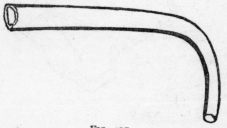

FIG. 40C.

foot-bellows and hand blow-pipe, with an oil lamp or a spirit lamp, or, as almost all old work was done, on a charcoal fire, with fans and small bellows.

The spirit lamp (fig. 40A) and the oil lamp (fig. 40B), with the mouth blow-pipe (fig. 40C), generally are only suitable for small work, as the amount of heat required for work of any size is very great. But a

very great deal of work can be done with
the spirit or oil lamp. Both are very easy
to manage, only in the case of the oil
lamp more care is needed to keep a good
flame and to avoid smoking the work.
It is most important to acquire freedom
in the use of the blow-pipe, and to this
end the student should practise with two
sizes of blow-pipe—one for large and one
for small work.

CHAPTER XII

Settings—The Kinds of Stones to Use—Close Settings
—Setting the Stone—Open Settings—Paved
Settings.

IN choosing stones to set, avoid those that
are cut into facets. Select those that
are rounded or cabochon cut; if you can
do so, use stones that are cut by Eastern
lapidaries. The Oriental has an eye for
colour and form, and has no foolish fears
of so-called flaws. The stones rejected
by the jeweller are almost always well
worth the attention of the artist. See
that those you buy have a fairly level bed
for the setting, and that the stone is well
bevelled, so that the setting will hold

when it is rubbed over. Settings may be open or closed. The closed setting is a box, the upper edge of which is rubbed over the stone. The open setting may be a mere rim without a bottom, or a circlet of claws. Or the two may be combined, and a close setting set in a large open-work setting of branches and leaves, as in early French or German work.

In incrusted work the stones are let into recesses carved out below the surface of the metal. The edges of the opening are then drawn up to the stone by careful work with punch and burnishers. This method is common in Indian and Persian work.

To Make a Close Setting.—Cut a band of silver, size 5 or 6 metal gauge, somewhat

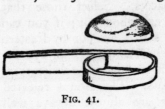

wider than the intended height of the setting, to allow for filing level and rubbing over, bend the strip

FIG. 41.

round so that it fits closely over the stone (fig. 41). When you have fitted the band closely to the contour of the stone, cut off the superfluous metal, file the juxtaposed

98

ends true, tie the setting round with fine
binding-wire so that the ends meet (fig.
41A); take the borax brush
and paint the joint, cut a
paillon of solder,[1] dip it
in the borax, and lay it
on the joint. Then put the setting thus
charged on the wire mop or on a piece
of charcoal, warm it in the flame, and
when the borax has ceased boiling direct

FIG. 41A.

FIG. 42.

the tip of the blue flame on the joint
and the setting. The solder should run
almost immediately. If it has flushed

[1] The solder for the band of the setting should be harder
running than the rest.

99

the joint, the setting may be cooled and made true by tapping it round with a light hammer on a taper steel mandrel (fig. 42)—an old steel cotton-spindle makes an excellent mandrel—and the bottom edge filed flat. Then take a piece of silver, 6 or 8, according to the use to which you intend to put the setting, and a little larger all round than it, scrape the surface clean, tie the setting on with binding-wire (fig. 43), and anoint the surfaces to be joined as before, and set a few paillons round the joint and proceed as before. When the joint is complete, file off the

FIG. 43.

superfluous metal, and you will have a box which just takes the stone. This, if the work is properly done, gives the simplest form of setting. If desired, a bearing for the stone can be made by fitting a concentric but narrower band inside this. The stone is now supported all round, and the work of rubbing over is made much easier. The edges of the setting are then filed true, the superfluous metal at the base cut away, and the whole made clean and workmanlike. Settings

100

can be grouped together and united by
filagree-work to form brooches, clasps,
necklaces; but this will be described in
a later chapter.

Open settings, collets, or crown settings,
are made by taking a strip of thick metal
(10 gauge), bending it a little smaller than
the stone, and soldering as before. Then
take a sharp graving-tool, wet the point,
and cut away the metal inside the top

FIG. 44.

edge so as to leave the ledge about a six-
teenth down in which the stone must fit
(fig. 44). Then take a small file and form
the setting into leaves or claws, or whatever you wish, taking care first to block
out the main forms, always remembering
to leave enough metal at the top to hold
the stone. The outer surface of the claws,
or leaves may be carved with the round
gravers to whatever shape is desired (fig.
45). Or the drill may be used to produce

perforated patterns below the line of the base of the stone; in fact, there is no end to the variety of forms which may be pro-

FIG. 45.

duced in this way. The main thing is to secure the stone firmly in its place; unless this is done in the first shaping of the setting, it cannot be done properly afterwards.

Paved Settings. — These are settings scorpered out of the solid metal. The

FIG. 46.

method is one which has been much abused, but is yet capable of much beauty when properly applied. The outline of the stone is marked on the plate, the ground is then carefully cut away with the scorper until the stone just fits in its place (fig. 46). You then cut a border round the stone, sloping away out-

102

wards as wide as you wish, keeping this
border highest next the stone. When
the remainder of the
work is finished,
cleaned, and stoned
and polished, the

Fig. 47.

gem is put in its place, and held there
while the metal is burnished up against it
(fig. 47). This work requires great care
and patience, for if not properly done the
stone will quickly become loose. This
method can only be applied to the harder

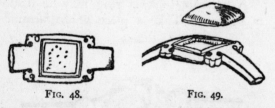

Fig. 48.   Fig. 49.

stones. Figs. 48 and 49 show a paved
setting used in the centre of a ring, with
tiny pierced fleur-de-lys in the angles.

103

CHAPTER XIII

Rings

THE simplest form is a hoop of flattened wire or a band of metal coiled round a mandrel and soldered. This is the foundation of more elaborate forms.

A pleasant-looking ring may be made as follows. Take a piece of half-round

FIG. 50.

silver wire about $\frac{1}{16}$ inch wide, solder two fine wires lengthwise down each side of it, then weave this into a knot leaving an opening in the centre (fig. 50). At every one of the crossings of the knot solder a tiny bead of silver made by

104

cutting off snippets of metal and running them up into beads on a piece of charcoal; then take a small stone, a garnet or an opal or a chrysoprase, and set it in a close setting. Fit the setting inside the opening in the knot (fig. 51), and solder it there, taking care to leave room for rubbing the setting over the stone. Then make the band of the same compound wire, and solder two V-shaped bands to it as wide apart as the width of the knot; then solder the knot in between these, arranging the arms of the V's so that they run in with the lines of the

FIG. 51.

knots; cover the joints with beads, either single or grouped three, four, or five together, or with single beads flattened out on the stake, then pickle the ring, stone it with small bits of Water of Ayr stone, or slips of slate, or with pointed slips of boxwood dipped in pumice powder and oil. Then polish it on the lathe with the scratch-brush, and after setting the stone finish on the buff with rouge.

You can vary this pattern to almost

105

any extent by using different sections of wire and different arrangements of the knots and beads; *e.g.*, the central wire instead of being round can be flat with hollow notches filed out of each side before the side wires are soldered to it. The knot can be made more complete by interlacing thinner wires in and out of the others, or you can add twigs and leaves in the interspaces.

FIG. 52.

To Make Leaves.—Take a wire of the thickness you require the twig to be, heat the end in the blow-pipe flame, plunge it in the borax, then direct the blue flame on the tip. The wire will quickly melt and run up into a bead (fig. 52). As soon as the bead forms, plunge the wire into water, and after flattening on the stake you can file it into whatever shape you please. Groups

106

of three or five of these soldered together and the leaves joined at the tips by tiny beads look very well (fig. 52) when combined with knot work of flat wire.

Another form of ring is the filagree table ring (fig. 53). Take any small irregular stone and make a setting. Take

filagree wire, or fine twisted wire flattened in the rollers (see fig. 55) will do as well, twist up the wire into a simple wreathed symmetrical pattern. Then take a piece of modelling wax— not modelling paste, that corrodes the silver—fix the setting upright in it and arrange the wire wreath round it. Have ready some flattened beads, group them into simple patterns with the wreath (see fig.), and press ever so lightly into the wax. (Fig. 54 shows another form of table filagree with a pearl centre.) Then mix a small quantity of fine plaster of Paris and place a good body of it over the whole group; leave it to set and when

FIG. 53.

107

quite dry and hard remove the wax carefully. The silver will be found fixed in the plaster. Remove the plaster with a brush from between the joints and around the setting, but do this without disturbing the pattern in any way. Dry the plaster thoroughly in an oven or by the fire, then paint borax on the setting

and over the crossings of the wire, and everywhere you wish to solder. Put paillons in the necessary places and play the flame over the whole gradually so that any chance moisture may be driven off. If this is done too suddenly the plaster may fly into pieces.

FIG. 54.

You will then direct the flame on the setting and the wreath until the solder has run everywhere. Then turn up a ring out of a strip of silver and solder it. Take a coil of wire twisted from right to left and another twisted from left to right and a length of plain wire a size or two larger. Boil out the band in dilute acid, coil the plain wire round the middle

108

of the band and solder it, coil the twisted
wires on either side of it and solder
them, using very small paillons of solder,
as if much is used the coils of twist will
be filled up. When the bare ring is
finished thus far, boil it out, clean it
in a little pickle, also the setting and
the filagree. Take a piece of flatted wire
—twisted wire or ordinary round wire
passed once or twice through the rollers
(fig. 55)—and bend it to the outline of
the table of filagree, and after tying it
on with fine wire,
solder it to the edge
to give strength.
Then tie this table
to the ring with wire and solder the two
together, and arrange branch pieces of
flatted wire or double rows of twist wire,
so as to strengthen the junction of the
ring with the table (fig. 53). These
branch pieces will go from side to side
of the ring behind the filagree, and their
junction with the ring should be covered
with a shield cut out of thin metal, or a
flatted bead, or a knot of twist wire, or a
group of grains like a flower. The main
thing is that the joint must be covered.
The junction of the branch pieces with the
table of filagree will then be strengthened

FIG. 55.

109

by round grains soldered in. It is important to remember in all ring designs that there must be no spiky projections; all must be rounded and smooth, and pleasant to the touch. As the field for the display of workmanship is only the upper area of the first joint of the finger, all ornament should be confined mainly to that space. Many things look well in

FIG. 56.

a sketch which look ridiculous on the finger. It is best therefore to build up the effect on the ring itself, using a little hard wax to hold the pieces of silver and whatever stones you may use together. You will soon find out what effect is best if you remember that every design must have three principal features—the ring proper, the junction, and the bezel. Many old rings were carved out of the solid metal (fig. 56). To make a ring of this kind, you will first cast an ingot of the shape you require (fig. 57), or hammer a cast bar into the rough form; then anneal the metal, and put it on the pitch. Then sketch on the design in black water-colour with a brush, and have ready

a few chisels of various sizes made by
sharpening a few tracers on an oilstone.
Outline the ornament or the figure with
a small round-edged tracing-tool, and
afterwards cut away the groundwork with
a rounded chisel. Then, with ordinary
chasing tools, you can model the surface
of the leaves and twigs or the figure as

FIG. 57.

much as you please. Remember always
to have a bit of the natural foliage near
you as a guide; never do anything in
the way of ornament without reference to
nature or without having made a careful
detailed study of the plant or form you
intend to use. You will have quite
enough to do to overcome the technical
difficulties without having also to puzzle
your head over the form.

This is a rule which should never be
neglected ; you must learn the form before
you can use it. Avoid sprawling lines ;
let leaves and twigs be well knit together,
let all the lines lead the eye to some central
point. You must not imitate but translate.

III

All art is translation from one state into another, and the manner of the translation reveals the quality of the artist.

When you have modelled the wreath or the knot as much as you wish, you can then carve the remainder of the band with a running wreath or a chevron, or with a graver hollow out symmetrical cuts all round the band. File and scrape the inside smooth; polish with a ringstick, which is a taper rod of wood covered with chamois leather, and charged with rouge.[1]

CHAPTER XIV

NECKLACES should be designed on a circle of 4½-in. diameter, and all pendants should

---

[1] Rings (hollow) can be chased up after the lining has been soldered in by boiling the ring (after a tiny hole has been pierced in the lining) in a strong solution of borax or alum. This makes a strong foundation for chasing, and can be removed by boiling in water afterwards.

be arranged on radial lines. No pendants
should go beyond the semicircle or they
will hang awkwardly on the shoulder when
worn.

Cut a circle out of thin copper or brass
4½ in. in diameter. Have ready the stones
you desire to use, and some flattened wire
or rolled twist. Make a few flattened
beads, and then sketch out the design
which suggests itself when you have arranged the stones according to their preciousness and colour. You will find that
the mere symmetrical arrangement of the
stones round the circle will suggest almost
instantly any number of methods of treatment. Choose what seems the simplest,
and twist up your wire to form knots or
wreaths round the stones (fig. 58), and
then arrange for the chains and loops
which will be needed to link all up together.

Avoid the use of shop-made chains;
they spoil the effect of the most carefully
devised necklace. The only chain possible
to use is that called Venetian chain, but
even that is not quite satisfactory. The
way to secure a good effect of chain-work
is to coil up the links yourself. This is
best done by taking a piece of flattened

H   113

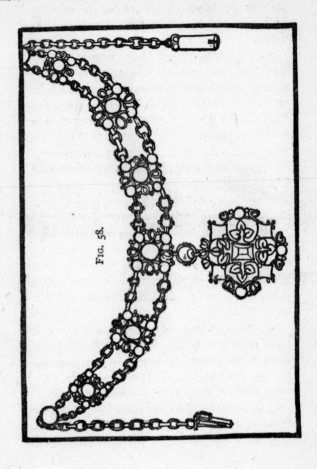

FIG. 58.

wire, oblong in section, with the edges rounded off with the file. This is to serve as the mandrel, and its size is regulated by the size of the links you desire. Wrap a strip of thin paper spirally round the mandrel, and secure it at each end with a few turns of binding-wire. Then take the wire, which may be simple or compound as described for rings, and fix the mandrel

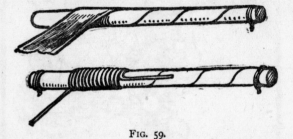

FIG. 59.

in a bench vice if the wire to be coiled is thick, or in a hand-vice if it be thin. Coil the wire spirally round the mandrel very closely and regularly until you have used as much wire as you require (fig. 59). Heat the whole with the blow-pipe on the mop until the paper is charred away. You can now withdraw the mandrel from the coil, which would be impossible were

115

the paper not used. With a jeweller's fret-saw cut off the links lengthwise down the spiral, keeping this cut as clean as possible. You can then coil on another mandrel of different, *e.g.* circular, section and slightly larger another kind of wire, simple or compound, as may be necessary

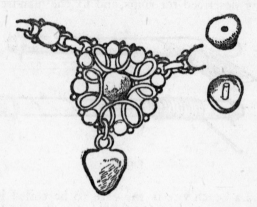

FIG. 60.

to give contrast to the first series, and saw these apart in like manner. You will then loop the two together in such lengths as you may need for connecting the various features of the necklace (fig. 62); and you must solder each link separately on the mop, taking care by using a small blow-pipe and a small flame to confine the heat to the link you are soldering.

FIG. 61.

A pleasant effect can be produced by setting rough pearls or stones in a background of wire filagree (see fig. 60) or wreath-work of leaves and twigs (figs. 61 and 61A). It must be made as follows:—Take the stones you have selected, make either close or open settings, whichever you prefer, and set them round the metal circle. If you choose rough pearls or pearl blisters, take small pieces of silver, size 5 or 6, and dome them up with a rounded doming-punch, either on the lead-block or on the doming-block, to fit the backs of the pearls. If the pearls are irregular in shape, you must shape the metal backs with rounded punches on lead. Having fitted each pearl with a back, you can either file away the back until it can hardly be seen from the front,

FIG. 61A.

117

or you can keep the edge well to the front and file it into symmetrical shapes, or you can border it with twisted wire or

FIG. 62.

with wire bent into a rippled shape (see fig. 63) and soldered   Having made the backs for the pearls or the settings for the stones, arrange them round the metal circle—naturally keeping the best and largest stone or pearl for the centre. Bend up some flattened wire into woven knots, as shown in the diagram, and solder the cups or settings on the wreath.   Then make long interwoven loops of wire with circles or squares or groups of beads soldered at the crossings (fig. 64). This is not only to strengthen the work, but to give the necessary con-

FIG. 63.

trast of broad, simple surfaces, with the wreathing lines of the loops and backgrounds of the stones or pearls. Then make oval links, as described above, and loop the links all together.

118

You will need a pendant for the centre.
This can either be made out of a group
of pearls or stones with a tiny panel of
repoussé or enamel in the centre, or it may
be a small group of figure-work, if the
student is advanced enough to do this.

You will now make the chain. This
should consist of links, repeating the
forms of the links in the central portion;
these will afterwards be joined together
by small subsidiary links. A very pretty

FIG. 64.

link is made with groups of grains or
beads soldered on both sides of the link
(see fig. 66). These, alternately with loops
coiled up out of flattened wire, look very
sparkling and pleasant when polished.
These grained loops must be so arranged
that the points are not likely to stick into
the skin or to scratch when the necklace
is worn. They must all lie flat, and the
connecting loops must be smooth. The
catch must next be made. Take a piece

119

of brass wire 4 or 5 inches long, oblong in section, ⅛ in. broad, file the angles until it is nearly oval in section, or you may pass a piece of round wire through the rolling-mill. This is to serve as the mandrel (fig. 65). Bend a slip of No. 5 metal ½ inch wide, so that it fits round the mandrel closely, and solder the join. On one end you will solder a bit of the same size metal and a ring on the centre of this; at the other end you will file a notch half-way across the tube, and in this notch solder a narrow strip of silver, leaving a slot between the tube and

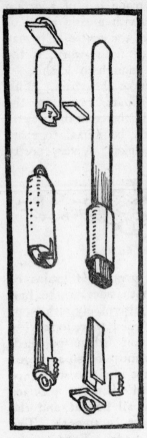

FIG. 65.

the edge of the strip; this is to take the tongue of the catch. In the centre of the strip you will file out a notch dividing it entirely, and also the end of the tube for about $\frac{1}{8}$th of an inch. Then take a slip of silver as wide as the tube and half as thick, solder a plate of No. 5 metal at right angles on the end, then take another slip the same width as the first, and solder the two together at the opposite end to the right-angled plate. This is the tongue of the catch, and you must leave a space between the end plate and the end of this last slip or tongue, so that when it is pushed into its place the tongue may spring up and catch behind the slotted end plate of the body of the catch. A tiny slip of silver is now prepared which will just fit in the slot already filed in the body of the snap; this must be soldered on the end of the tongue. Now try if it will fit the catch, and if not, file the sides of the slot neatly and truly until the tongue slips in quite easily and springs up and holds the catch in its place and does not wriggle about. You will then file it up true and clean when, having linked one part on each end of the necklace and soldered the joins the whole is complete.

121

You will then boil out the whole necklace in dilute acid until it comes out quite white. Afterwards polish the silver-work with the scratch-brush, using a little stale beer as a lubricant. Next wash it out in warm water, set the stones, and rub the settings over with the burnisher. At the same time you may burnish bits of the ornament, the loops, and particularly the flattened beads. Then repolish the whole with rouge to a brilliant surface.

You may wish to make a necklace entirely of silver. We will suppose it is to be a garland of roses. Now, for metal-work, it is important that all the natural forms you employ should be generalised; that is to say, while you cannot study too closely the method of growth and the characteristic shapes of the leaves, buds, flowers, and fruit, you must avoid slavish imitation of accidental forms or the minute details of the growth. In your studies be as minute as you please, you cannot be too painstaking; put in everything you see. But when you translate these studies into work, learn to leave out. The artist is known as much by what he omits as by what he puts in his work. He seeks forms typical of his subject and yet suitable to his material.

Now, for our immediate purpose a rose-bush is an assemblage of more or less symmetrically arranged masses of leaves, each leaf being a symmetrical group of five subsidiary leaves. Relieved against this mass of leaves we have large and small bossy forms, the roses and the buds. For our necklace the simplest way is to arrange the rose boughs in a series of panels of pierced repoussé, alternately square and roundish (figs. 66 and 67), the panels afterwards connected by loops and beads. In these panels the roses and buds will be in high relief, the leaves and branches in lower and flatter relief, so that when the whole is polished the roses and buds will shine out brilliantly as jewels.

FIG. 66.

Take your circle, as before, and lay it on a bit of paper or on a sheet of wax rolled out. See how large you can make the panels, and how many you may require. Take a piece of silver, size 8, and outline the shapes of the panels, and sketch on it the main branches and mark the position of the

123

bosses of roses. Lay the metal face down on a thick piece of cork or cork-matting and punch out these roses from the back, and then punch out the smaller group of buds, distributing them carefully so as to get a sparkling effect. Then, after heating the pitch, lay the metal down after oiling the under surface. You will now outline the leaves and branches, keeping the arrangement as symmetrical and as simple

Fig. 67.

as possible. Avoid curly leaves, coiling branches, wormlike roots, and squirming forms. Keep the drawing of the leaves clear and accurate and decided. When you have done this, then outline the roses and draw the petals on the bosses, either open or partly closed. Then with a sharp tracer outline the spaces to be pierced, which will probably be the whole of the ground, and then when you have done all you can to the repoussé, take the silver off the pitch, clean it and pickle it. Then lay each panel on its face and file away the ridges made by the outlining tracer, and soon the tiny

124

scraps of the ground will drop out and
the ornament will show clear against the
light. Next take a piece of silver for the
back of the panel, size 4 or 5, a little larger
all round than your panel, dome it up very
slightly so that it may press against the
backs of the twigs and leaves. When it
fits scrape the surface all over and tie the
two securely together ; use plenty of borax
between the joints, tack the back and
front together in two or three places round
the edge and in the centre. When the
solder has run, press the joints closely together wherever the metal has been warped
by the heat, or wherever the joint may have
been imperfectly fitted or secured. Then
clean the whole in acid and recharge with
borax and with enough but not too much
solder, and see that the solder flushes
well under and into all the joins. You
can then pierce the ground out with a
drill and fret-saw. Do not saw too closely
to the ornament, leave a narrow fillet to
be filed away afterwards, and before cutting away the waste metal round the edge
coil up some rings out of 14 wire and
solder them on the back plate in contact with the panel where they are required. If these rings are simply soldered

against the panel they are apt to pull off after a certain amount of wear. To loop these panels up together, you will require loops or links which carry out the design of the main panels. These may be either roses with a few leaves, or boughs twined up into closely knit bosses.

When the circlet is completed, you will make the catch, and the whole, after pickling, will be ready to be stoned and polished. If you wish to make a pendant for this necklace, it must not merely be an elaborated panel, but should have some central point of interest. You may either read "The Romaunt of the Rose" and take thence whatever suggestion most appeals to you, or you may prefer to put a nightingale singing in the middle of a bower of leaves (fig. 68). The latter will be the least difficult, as the former supposes a knowledge of the figure,

FIG. 68.

126

though you might make a little gateway
with towers to the garden of the Rose,
which could be made very interesting.

To Make the Nightingale.—First go and
watch one singing. There are happily
numberless woods and copses near London
in which the nightingale may be heard and
seen at almost any time of the day. Take
an opera-glass and find the spot most frequented by the birds and least frequented
by humans; sit motionless and watch
them while they sing. If you have not
seen one before, you will never forget the
first sight of the little brown-backed, grey-
breasted bird against the sky and leaves,
with head thrown back and his throat
throbbing in an ecstasy of song. Make
as many sketches as you can, and when
you get home take a piece of silver, size 8,
—of fine silver if you are going to enamel,
or standard if left from the tool, and it
must be a good deal larger than the size
you propose to make the bird—anneal
it, sketch the outline the reverse way, and
with a rounded doming-punch boss out
the metal as much as you can on the cork
pad. Then fasten the same domed punch
in the vice, and after again annealing,
take a boxwood or horn mallet and beat

127

the metal still further round, until the rough relief is as high as the thickness through the body of the bird. Re-anneal the metal, lay it on the pitch, and shape the bird carefully with chasing and repoussé tools, driving the metal gradually round behind the back of the bird, taking care that you do not crack it in the process. You will find it possible to get the body quite in the round save for a narrow opening at the back. When you have modelled the surface as you wish, cut away the ground and solder a piece of metal over the opening, taking care, if there be no other escape for the air, to drill a small hole where it will least be seen. Then you will take another piece of metal, size 6, or a little less, and make the bower of leaves or branches within which the bird is to be set. You must keep it wreath-like and clear and simple in outline without any spikiness or too great irregularity of surface. It should be made double, the pattern on the back being developed from that on the face. The two can then be filed and fitted together, and pickled and soldered.

When the wreath is complete you can tie the bird in its place and solder it to the bough you have prepared for it. When the work is clean you can then take a rounded graver and a cement-stick, and after fastening the bird and wreath on the wax, you can sharpen up the modelling of the leaves, cut away superfluous solder, and make the whole clean and workmanlike. The wreath can be hung to the necklace by one or two chains or loops. You will

FIG. 69.

probably find that six loops of flat wire enriched with twist soldered round alternate links, with a rose boss in the centre of the six links, will be sufficient (fig. 69). The loops must be fairly broad and not too long, or the pendant will twist about and will not hang truly. Then loop the whole necklace temporarily together to see the effect. It should hang in one even curve, and any irregularity must be corrected by lengthening or shortening links wherever necessary. You will probably find that a second drop or subordinate pendant is needed beneath the bird. Make a pear-shaped group of leaves and roses in two halves (fig. 70), solder them together with a loop at the top, and hang this by means of three or five links to the wreath.

When it all seems as complete as you can make it, put it all in the pickle and leave it till quite white and clean. Stone it carefully and polish on the lathe with the scratch-brush and stale beer. Then wash clean with soap suds and hot water, and dry it in the sawdust. It will look staring and unpleasantly white and bright. This defect can be removed by brushing it over with a hot solution of ammonia sulphide in water. Take care that it does not get into the setting or the effect of the stone may be entirely spoilt. When the surface gets as dark as you wish, wash it clean in hot water, and polish it by hand with a wash-leather and a little rouge.

FIG. 70.

CHAPTER XV

Brooches—Suggestions for Design—Mounting—The Making of Compound Twists—The Joint and Catch.

BROOCHES should be kept rather small, and be designed on the same principles as

130

pendants. The back, however, should always be smooth, and if possible somewhat concave. We will suppose you have a moonstone which you wish to set. Choose some poetical subject suggested by the stone. If I were doing it I should probably reason in this way:—"The moonstone suggests Diana. Her symbol is a stag. The subject shall be a running stag bearing the moon in his antlers." But this is only one way of looking at the subject; the student must choose his own. What is personal to one may be an affectation in another, and affected art is bad art.

Suppose, however, that you choose to do a stag. Make a drawing of a stag running, or standing sidewise with his head thrown back or turned towards the spectator. We will suppose you make him standing with his head and antlers thrown back. You can either set the stone behind the antlers, like a moon rising behind trees, or you can use the antlers as part of a setting. Having made the drawing of the stag as you wish, take a piece of silver of suitable size and gauge, 8 or 10 if for high relief, 6 or 7 if for lower relief. Fit your design within some simple set form, a circle, an oval, or square, and

131

beat the stag out in relief. Make the
setting for the stone and fit it into its
place carefully, and if the stone is to be
set in the background, arrange the horns
so that they will take the setting of the
stone, and see that the stone is placed
nicely in relation to the rest of the enclosing
space. When the repoussé is done, boil it
clean, and if the ground is to be pierced,
make a back as described for the silver
necklace. If it is not pierced, dome
slightly a piece of No. 5 silver sufficiently
large to leave a $\frac{1}{4}$-inch margin all round.
After the back and front are tacked together, drill a couple of small holes, one
at each end of the horizontal diameter
a little within the places for the joint and
catch. This is to let the air escape, otherwise the imprisoned air expands, and either
bursts the back off, or distorts the front
by bulging it out in its weakest place.

You will now require a border. Take a
round wire, size 12, pass it through the flat-
tening-roller or hammer it into a ribbon, or
draw a piece of round wire through a draw-
plate with oblong holes. Take a length
of smaller wire, about 4 in the metal
gauge, double it and twist up tightly
from right to left; twist another piece

132

from left to right. Take two lengths of
copper wire, the size of the silver wire before it was flattened, and tie one on each
side of the silver ribbon with iron binding-
wire. Then fix one end of this compound
wire in the vice and one end in a hand-
vice or a pair of slides, and twist the whole
until the spiral is as close as you wish it.
You can then remove the copper wires and
replace with the silver twists, and after
tying them in their place, you can solder
them here and there, using small paillons
and taking care not to fill up the twists
with solder. Now boil, clean, and solder
it round your panel as a frame.

Instead of doing this you can make a
circle of small stars, either in repoussé
round the panel, or you can make a
number of groups of grains and solder
them round. The latter has the more
sparkling effect, but it takes much longer
to do. When the border is made, file the
surplus metal from the back and round
the edge, and it will be ready to receive
the joint or catch. Take a piece of thick,
half-round wire and bend it into the shape
of a C with a long tail (C); then file the
bottom of the tail flat, and afterwards
solder it in position on the brooch near,

but not actually on the edge. Next you must make the hinge for the pin. Take a piece of fine tube, about size 12 in the

metal gauge, and solder a short length, about ⅜th inch long, on a slip of No. 5, a little larger each

FIG. 71.

way (fig. 71). Then take a piece of stout silver wire and run the end up into a good-sized bead (fig. 72). Flatten the bead and file it into shape as shown. Upon the flat side of this you will solder another and shorter length of tube (fig. 73). File out of the centre of the first

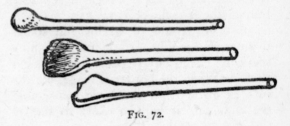

FIG. 72.

tube a space wide enough to take the tube on the end of the pin (see fig. 73A). When the two fit perfectly, take another piece of No. 5 and solder it at one side

134

of the bottom joint (see fig. 73A) so that
the two lengths of tube are in the angle
of an L. The last piece helps to make

FIG. 73.

the spring of the pin. The flat end of the
pin catches against this; the pin being bent
down under the catch is held in place by
the elasticity of the metal (fig. 74). Pins
made of 9-carat gold are very much better
than silver pins; they are harder, and have
more spring in them. The joint, when
filed up true and clean, can be soldered
in place. The whole can now be boiled
out and scratch-brushed, and the stone set.
If you have a
close setting, it
is best to back
the stone with a
piece of white
foil to give it
greater brilli-
ancy. Another

FIG. 73A.

way of setting stones in the background of
any panel, is to beat out a hollow from
the back into which the stone exactly fits.

135

You will then pierce out all of this except a narrow piece just sufficient to retain the stone firmly. You will then turn up a narrow setting of thin silver and file the edge either wavy or scolloped or ser-

FIG. 74.

rated, and solder it in behind as shown (fig. 75). This forms a subsidiary setting,

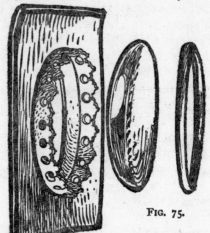

FIG. 75.

and when all is complete the stone can be dropped into its place and a piece of round

136

wire, bent to the curve of the setting, can
then be fitted in behind the stone, and the
wavy, scolloped, or serrated edges of the
setting bent over the wire and burnished
until the stone is set quite firmly. The
advantage of this is, that the work
on the background can be carried round
the setting without any of the awkward
joins which are almost impossible to avoid
when a separate setting is soldered in or
upon the ground. At the same time
you must not make the work look as if a
hole had been made in the metal and a
stone dropped casually in. The setting
must be frankly made to look like a setting, and the foliage or branches in the
background must be made to lead up to
the setting as the culminating point of the
whole jewel.

CHAPTER XVI

Pendants—Things to be Avoided—Suggestions for
Design—The Use of Enamel—Setting the Enamel—The Hoop for the Pendant—Polishing.

PENDANTS should not be large or sprawl-
ling. Points, projections, and roughnesses
should be avoided. The lines of the

ornament should tend towards the centre
or to some point of interest within the
outline. The back should be made interesting as well as the front. My method
of design is to make each jewel enshrine
some story or symbol. I try to make the
ornament allusive to the gem, to its legen-
dary history, to its qualities, or to the
ideas suggested by it. For example, you
take an aqua-marine; the name itself, no
less than the colour, at once suggests things
of the sea. Any other method is permis-
sible if the student is sincere. He must
follow whatever inspiration is given him
at all costs, and in spite of everything.
The design now suggested is merely a peg
on which to hang the technical description.
Lay your stone or stones on a bit of silver,
and draw fishes swimming spirally to or
from the stone as a centre; make studies
of fish, avoiding grotesque or extraordinary
forms; pay great attention to the bony
structure of the head and the set of the
fins. Look at any Japanese drawings of
fish you can get hold of, and follow their
methods.

After you have made the setting for the
stone, draw the fish on the silver, boss the
whole well out from the back, arrange a

138

hollow for the setting of the stone and fairly
deep hollows between the fish to be filled
with enamel, and let the outlines of the fish
be fairly undercut to give good hold for the
enamel. Put a range of spiral curls rather
high in relief all round to make a frame,
and let the tip of the spirals lip over the
bodies of the fish so that they are encircled
by waves (fig.
76). When
the repoussé is
finished, you
must arrange
for the back.
You can have
it all in enamel
like a sea, or
you can put
a silver ship
with sails on
enamel waves.

FIG. 76.

A modern sailing ship is still as beautiful a thing as men make nowadays, and
you should make a careful drawing of
one. Take care that it fills the panel
well, and raise it and chase it until it
is as complete as you can make it. If
you intend to put an enamel sea, you
must prepare a sunken ground wherever

139

the enamel is to come, and the edges of the ground must be undercut, so that the silver itself frames the enamel. Nothing looks worse than enamel melting away into modelled work without a line to frame it and keep it in its proper place in the composition. Enamel is not a kind of paint which can be applied anywhere as a means of hiding inferior work ; it must be treated as a precious material, and employed in small quantities. The modern tendency to cover large surface with enamel vulgarises the material, making it look like so much coloured varnish, and this without any corresponding advantage. You will then clean the metal by boiling out in acid, and wherever the enamel comes, the ground and the back of the metal also is to be scraped quite clean and bright all over.

Choose two or three good rich enamels, ranging from dark to pale sea-green, and grind it up fairly fine, and wash it well till all milkiness disappears ; then paint the back of each plate, wherever there is to be enamel in front, with gum tragacanth and water, and dust the backing (see chapter on Enamel Work) all over. Shake off the surplus, and leave to dry. Then take the ground greens, add a tiny drop

of gum to each mixture, fill in the spaces
left for the sea, shading the greens from
dark at the edge to light at the centre,
making the lightest green a little darker
than the central stone, because everything
must lead up to that. Then fire carefully
in the muffle until the enamel flows smooth
and shining, remove from the furnace, and
cool slowly in a sand bath or in front of
the stove.

When cool, you can remove any irregularities of surface with a corundum file
and water. If necessary, re-fire to get all
smooth and bright. You will now have
to arrange the fitting of the two together.
Take a piece of 10 silver, a little larger
than the outline of the pendant, mark
the outline all round with a point, leaving projections where loops come, then
saw out the centre leaving only a band
$\frac{1}{8}$-inch wide. Cut a narrow band of No. 5
silver, bend it round the outline, and
when it fits solder the ends together, and
solder the whole to the plate you have
sawn out, so that you have, as it were, a
skeleton setting. Treat the other side
in a similar way. File the setting into
a wave-like line, and, after soldering two
strong loops to the central plate, file away

141

the surplus metal, and make the whole
setting smooth to the touch and pleasant
to look at. Take a fine drill, and, fixing
the front in place, drill a hole here and
there through the setting and the relief.
Do this with the back also. Make taper

pins of silver wire
to fit the holes,
and, after rubbing
the edges of the
setting over with a
burnisher, insert the
pins and press them
firmly home. Cut
them off close to the
setting, and take a
small graining-tool
(fig. 77) or a hollow-
headed punch, the
hollow of which is
not larger than the
head of the pin,
grain the point over

FIG. 77.

with a circular movement until the rough
head of the pin is well rounded. This fixes
the pin firmly in its place. You will now
need to make the loop, and a little knop
to act as a spreader for the suspending
chains. You may make the knop to

142

suggest the air. Draw a seagull with out-stretched downward drooping wings. You can see them any day about the bridges on the Thames. Beat it up from a bit of 7 or 8 silver, underneath you can place a band of curling waves. The ground can either be cut away or it can be ena-melled in different blues. If enamel is used, the silver must be fine silver; and you must solder on the back with 18-carat gold solder—other solder is apt to be destroyed in the firing.

If you prefer the pierced ground, cut it away with a metal saw, and solder the bird on a back of No. 5 thickness. Take care that the joins are all well flushed up with solder. Provide for suspension loops, coiled rings for the bottom, and a loop like this 𝒬 for the top loop, all soldered on the back plate. Cut the ground away again and file up the whole true, and clean and stone ready for polishing. The loop is made of a thick piece of metal, No. 8 or 10, shaped as in fig. 78, A. Take a rounded doming-punch and hollow it well out from the back (fig. 78, B). Take a pair of round-nosed pliers and bend it as in fig. 78, C, and solder the ends together. Have ready the coiled

143

rings, and solder them to the loop (see fig. 78, D), and fix a grain between the two for the sake of strength no less than for appearance. Make chain loops as before described, and beat up four little bosses. They may be shells or little coiled fishes; make them double, solder them together, solder loops top and bottom, and then loop the whole up temporarily to see how it hangs. After correcting any inequalities, solder all the chains together, then polish with the scratch-brush and beer, and afterwards finish with rouge. The enamel portion can be polished with putty powder and a little water.

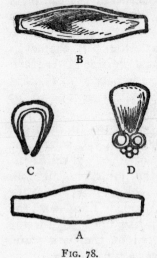

FIG. 78.

CHAPTER XVII

COMBS and other ornaments for the hair must be very light, and free from sharp angles or roughnesses. The required lightness is obtained either by using very thin metal, or by building up the design out of wire or filagree.

Let us take the simplest first, and make a long pin for the hair.

Take a rounded iron doming-punch and beat out two half-domes out of No. 2 or 3 silver, file the edges level, and solder the two halves together to make a complete ball. Leave a hole $\frac{1}{8}$ to $\frac{1}{4}$ inch wide in the centre of one of the half-domes and a smaller hole opposite this and fill it with pitch. Then warm the pitch-block, and wet the silver ball and press it into the pitch; then take a fine tracer and trace spiral lines round the dome, taking care not to drive the punch in too deeply; then

Hair Ornaments and Combs

FIG.
79.

with other punches chase
the surface into rounded
spiral ribs, either with a
narrow rib between each
pair, or simply a series of
rounded spirals. Next
take twisted wire, the
smallest size you can get,
and solder it into the hollows between the ribs.

This done, cut a piece of
stout silver wire 6 inches
long and file it into a taper
pin ; solder the chased ball
on the top of this pin so
that the end of the pin
projects very slightly.
Next take two rings of
wire, about $\frac{1}{4}$ inch in
diameter, solder the two
together crosswise, and
solder a small bead at the
top. Then solder this on
the top of a tiny piece of
round wire like a column,
and put a grain of silver
in each angle (see fig. 80) ;
then solder a tiny half-
dome of the silver on

146

the top of the large ball and the skeleton
ball and pillar on the top of this again.

Where the pillar meets the half dome
(fig. 81) you must put a ring
of fine wire to cover the joint
and make a neat finish. Now
take a piece of silver wire and
coil it on a mandrel, ½ inch in
diameter, about a dozen times.

FIG. 80.

Saw the rings apart and solder two
together as before described. At the
junctions you will solder two small rings
of flat wire, just large enough to let the
pin pass through both at the top and the
bottom. Cut the remaining rings in half,

FIG. 81.

and solder a half-ring in each
angle. Repeat this until you
have a skeleton sphere. It is
better to finish soldering at the
top of the sphere before pro-
ceeding to the other pole; and
when soldering the other ends,
it is better to cover the part already soldered with loam and water, or whiting and water; this will prevent the solder
from melting and the rings from falling to
pieces. The skeleton sphere can now be
strengthened by a row of tiny half-domes
and groups of six grains alternately; the

147

width of each half-dome and flower being
exactly the width apart of the ribs. Solder
one to the centre of each rib, and let all the
flowers and small half-domes be soldered to
each other. Next file away the crossing-
wires within the top and bottom rings, and
slip the completed ball into its place on
the pin; find the point at which it looks
best, and there solder a collar of wire on
the pin. You will now solder the skeleton sphere in its place, beginning at the
top. Protect the half not being soldered
with loam or whiting. When the upper
join is made, clean away the loam or whiting and boil the metal clean and white in
pickle. Scrape the joint bright, and slip
another ring on the pin to make a collar
underneath the spheres. Before proceed-
ing to solder, make two stout rings $\frac{1}{8}$ inch
inside measure, and tie them opposite each
other where the pin and sphere meet.
Then protect the rest of the work with
loam or whiting as before, and finish soldering. Next make six small hollow
spheres of No. 2 metal, and having coiled
up a number of small rings of fine wire
or fine twist, have ready a number of small
beads of silver, and solder the rings round
the outsides of the balls, and put a grain in

148

every alternate circle. Then solder a ring on
the top of each
ball, and make
six lengths of
fine chain as de-
scribed for neck-
laces, or simply
of circles of wire,
alternate twist
and plain, large
and small, and
loop three balls
on each loop as
shown in fig. 79.
Next hammer
the pin carefully
on a bent stake
to make it hard
and springy.
The whole can
now be cleaned
and polished.

*To Make a
Comb.*—Take a
strip of silver,
size 10 ordinary
gauge, and mark
out a simple
three or four-

FIG. 82.

149

pronged comb, as in the lower portion of
fig. 82. Leave a space of at least three-
quarters of an inch before you begin the
prongs. Then saw out the prongs and file
up the edges clean and smooth. Draw a
piece of fine tube, as described before, about $\frac{1}{16}$
inch in diameter, and sol-
der a length along the back
of these prongs as at A
in fig. 83.

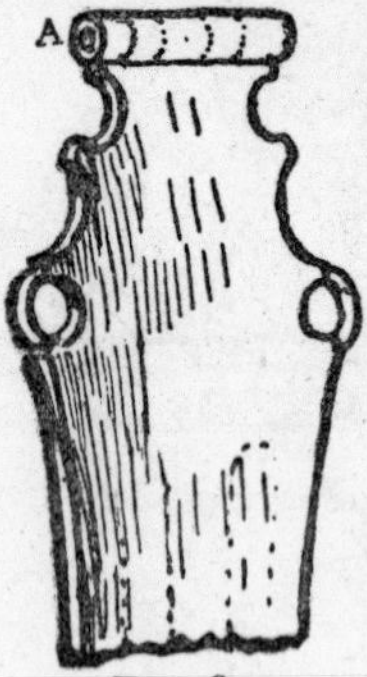

You will now require to
make the top of the comb.
The best way is to get a
few clear stones and arrange
them into a pleasant pattern,
with different shaped bosses
of metal and wreaths of filagree (fig.
84). This was an arrangement of aqua-
marines and pearls. The pearls should
be of irregular shapes, and drilled so
that they may be mounted as roses. First
make settings for the aqua-marines, and
solder them on a back-plate hammered
up into a domical section. Then make
strong twigs of thick wire hammered
taper and soldered together in a simple
interlacing pattern embracing the settings.
The pattern must not be too regular,

FIG. 83.

150

nor must the stones be of equal size or
colour.

When the main stems are soundly

FIG. 84.

soldered, take silver wire and make leaves
as before described, and solder them to-

gether in groups of five, with grains between each pair of leaves. Then make a
calix or skeleton setting for each of the
pearl roses, and solder a calix on the tip
of each principal twig, leaving enough of
the twig to pass through the pearl and be
riveted or grained over when the pearl is
fixed. This will be done when all the
soldering, cleaning, and polishing has been
completed. Hav-
ing fixed the posi-
tion of the roses,
you can now arrange
the groups of leaves
in order on the
stem, and solder
them, using loam or
whiting to protect
the joints. The

FIG. 85.

centre line of each leaf should be tan-
gential to the main curve (fig. 85).

When all the leaves have been soldered
on ycu will need to strengthen the bottom
plate both for the attachment of the hinge
and to bind up the settings for the stones
into a connected whole. Take a piece of
stout sheet-silver shaped as at B in fig. 68,
and, having filed it up smooth, tie it firmly
with wire, or strong clips of bent iron

152

wire, to the body of the comb. When the solder has flushed well in and around every joint boil the work clean in acid, and then file a groove with a rounded file along the bottom edge of the projecting tongue, and solder a tube of the same size as before into the groove; file spaces into each tube to receive the projections in the other. There should be not less than five joints—three above and two below (fig. 86). This

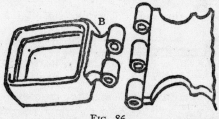

FIG. 86.

way of making the hinge is an easy one, but it is not the best, because it is almost impossible to file the joints of the hinge perfectly true and square without the joint tool. If you wish to spend more time on the work you can make the hinge in short lengths, as described for the casket hinge, and then, having slipped all the parts of the joint on a brass pin filed to fit, tie the head and the tang of the comb

153

together with the hinge between; then just
tack the tubes—three to the tang and two
to the head—with a tiny panel of solder
to each; do not flush the solder or you will
spoil the whole hinge by running the solder
into the joints. As a precaution you
should paint the inside of the tubes and the
faces of the joints with a little rouge and
water. When the parts are tacked, take
the work apart and solder it all firmly.

Next make two hollow balls, and solder
one to the end of a pin (fig. 87) which

exactly fits the
hinge, and,
having drilled
the other ball,

FIG. 87.

file a shoulder on the other end of the pin
just where it comes through the hinge.
When the comb is finally fitted together
the pin will be securely riveted over
the ball.

When the whole is stoned with Water
of Ayr stone and has been polished, you
may set the stones as before described.
In fixing the pearls you will need to use
shellac to cement them to their settings.
Take a stick of shellac, and after heating
one end in the gas flame, draw it out into
a long thread. Then heat the setting of

154

each stone, and wind a little of this thread of shellac round it. Warm the pearl, and run a little of the shellac in the hole; then, holding the setting and the pearl, one in each hand, over the flame, slip the pearl over the peg while the cement is liquid; when it is cold you can rivet the peg very carefully. If the pearls have not been drilled, you must drill them. To do this you will need a holder. It

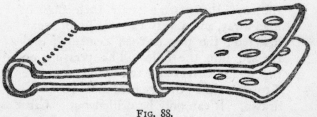

FIG. 88.

consists of a strip of brass bent as in fig. 88 and fixed in a hand-vice; a graduated series of holes is drilled through the two contiguous halves, the inner edges of the holes are then slightly countersunk to prevent injury to the pearl, a slip collar is made, and the instrument is complete.

Put the pearl you wish to drill in the pair of holes that most nearly fits it, slip the collar until the pearl is firmly held

155

You can now drill the hole without danger
of injuring the pearl or your own fingers.
There is no need to drill the pearl right
through, a well-made peg well cemented
will hold quite well, even if it only goes
half-way into the pearl. If the pearl is
specially valuable the peg may be keyed
on. This is done by drilling a hole and
making it larger at the bottom than at the
top. The peg used is made of two half-
round wires put together and soldered to
the cap, the two ends are then slightly
filed away, and a very tiny wedge of metal
inserted; the peg is then cemented and
pressed into the hole. The pressure on
the wedge drives the two halves of wire
outwards and the peg cannot be with-
drawn. It can only be drilled out. Care
is needed in doing this or the pearl may
be split.

CHAPTER XVIII

Bracelets—The Hammered Bracelet—The Hinge
Bracelet—The Band—The Snap—The Hinge
—Fitting the Joints—The Flexible Bracelet—
Cleaning and Burnishing.

Bracelets   BRACELET sizes range from 6¼ to 7 inches
in circumference.

156

Take a short length of thick silver wire about $\frac{3}{16}$ inch in diameter, anneal it, and flatten it out to a square section in the centre and fan-shaped and feather-edged at the ends (fig. 89).

When you have stretched it out to at least two inches longer than the circumference required, take a sharp chisel and divide the fan-shaped ends as shown in

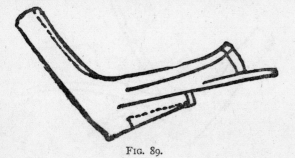

FIG. 89.

the diagram. Anneal the metal thoroughly, next open out the strips of metal and hammer them into a more regular taper. Do this to both sides, and anneal again. Mark out the right lengths of the bracelet, and bend the ends to a sharp angle, so that the tips of the ends will just reach the extremities of this line. Solder on each bend a short piece of silver the

157

thickness of the bracelet, making the
band of the bracelet just the right length,
and file up the ends true and clean. With
a pair of smooth, round-nosed pliers bend
up the taper twigs into simple scrolls
(fig. 90) and connect them with each
other by means of large beads made as
before described, and flattened with the

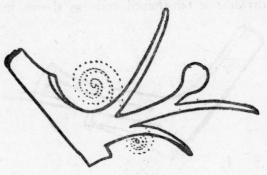

FIG. 90.

hammer on the square bench stake. When
this has been done to both sides, bend
the band round with two pairs of strong
pliers into the shape of a flattened circle.
To avoid marking the metal you must
make thin copper or brass shields to slip
over the jaws of the pliers. When the
curve is perfect, and the ends butt cleanly
together, take a small jewel, say a chryso-

158

prase, an opal, or a garnet. Make a box setting for it, and solder the setting on one side of the band, so that one-half of the setting will be on the band, the other half standing free. This will cover the junction of the ends and yet give the metal play, so that it can be slipped over the hand without difficulty (fig. 91). The outside of the bracelet may be hammered into a rounded or softly-bevelled section,

FIG. 91.

and the surface afterwards decorated with chasing-tools. This work will, of course, be done upon pitch. The inside of the bracelet must be scraped and filed clean and smooth and rounded, and all roughnesses removed from every part of the work with the Water of Ayr stone. It is now ready for whitening, stoning, and polishing. This done, the stone can be set and the final polishing given. When,

159

unless you wish to oxidise the work, which can be done as described elsewhere, the whole is finished.

To Make a Hinged Bracelet.—Cut an ellipse of the size required out of stout sheet brass (fig. 92). This is to serve as a guide when bending the band of the bracelet. Take two lengths of square silver wire and make two ovals to fit

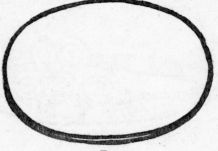

FIG. 92.

closely over the brass pattern. Solder the two ends together, and cut a narrow slip of No. 6 or 8 sheet-silver as broad as you wish to make the band. This can be decorated in repoussé with very simple patterns of symmetrically arranged dots or a simple running pattern.

Bend the band to fit the outside of the oval rings; tie the band and the rings

160

firmly together as in the diagram (fig. 93),
and solder the whole soundly together.
This makes the band of the bracelet. You
have now to make the hinge and snap.

To Make the Hinge or Joint.—Draw a
length of thin silver tube as wide as the
thickness of the bracelet edge, and another
length just to fit inside this tube. Drill
a hole through the edge wires of the

FIG. 93.

bracelet, and enlarge this with the needle
file, so that the larger tube will slip comfortably into its place. Now cut off a
short length of the larger tube a little
longer than the depth of the bracelet band,
and halve it lengthwise with the frame-
saw. Into one half solder two lengths of
the small tube, with a space between them
—each piece being a third as long as the

L

joint—and into the centre of the other half solder another piece of tube filed to

fit exactly between the first two (see fig. 94). Fit these two halves of the joint together after painting each with a little rouge and water to prevent them from sticking together while being soldered into the bracelet. Scrape the

FIG. 94.

outside of the tube quite clean, and tie it in place with binding - wire. See that the joint in the tube lies across the edge of the bracelet as in fig. 95. Put some small panels of solder on each side of the tube, and solder it without

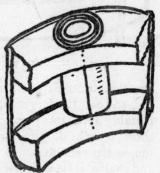

FIG. 95.

giving too much heat, or the solder may flush into the joint and spoil the work.

162

File the ends of the tube flush with the
edge of the bracelet. The snap is made
by cutting two strips of 8-gauge metal, one
for the back, and one for the face of the
snap. File the face into
the form at fig. 96. The
upper space is for the spring-
plate, the lower for the

FIG. 96.

bottom plate of the snap. For this latter
take a strip of 8 or 9-gauge silver, file
it to fit the lower slot B, and solder

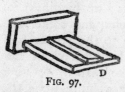

FIG. 97.

it at right angles to
the back-plate (see fig.
97). The spring-plate
is a narrow strip of
the same metal filed
to fit the groove C.

Solder the end of it to the bottom plate
at D so that the edge nearest the back-plate
is separated from the latter by a space
exactly the thickness of the
metal (fig. 98).

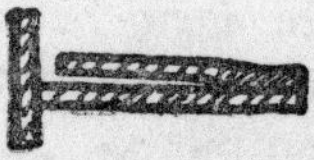

FIG. 98.

If you now file notches
in the band of the bracelet
lengthwise down the joint, and saw the
band through on the opposite side, the
bracelet will come in two, and can be
hinged up temporarily with a brass peg.
The snap-plates can now be soldered

163

to the other end. The plate A should first be soldered in position, a lining-plate, B, being soldered inside each half of the

FIG. 99.

bracelet (figs. 99, 100), and a slot filed at C to admit the thumbpiece of the snap. Fix the snap-plate carefully in place, rouge it, and tie it with wire. Scrape the back of the snap-plate and the end of the bracelet which abuts on this; tie binding-wire round the whole bracelet, and solder the back-plate of the snap to the proper half of the band. File the joint clean and smooth, and release the snap by pressing the point of a file or a knife upon the

spring-plate through the slot C. The thumbpiece, made of a strip of silver, can now be soldered in position, and the snap is complete. A loop may be soldered on each side for the attachment of the

FIG. 100.

safety-chain if you wish, but it is not absolutely necessary.

All the constructive enrichment of the band—as, for instance, a panel of filagree-

164

work, foliage, or set stones—should be done before the joint and snap are made, otherwise the bracelet may not snap or close properly.

How to Make a Flexible Bracelet.—Make a number of small half-domes out of No. 5 silver.

FIG. 101.

Take a silver wire, about 20 gauge, and coil it round a paper-guarded mandrel; anneal it, slip off the coils of wire, and with the saw cut off the loops one by one until you have a good number. Boil the rings clean, and arrange them together (see fig. 101) on a level piece of charcoal. Solder them all together, and solder a half-dome in the

FIG. 102.

middle and a grain in the intersections of the circles. Make a number of these links, say twenty. Make a similar number with groups of three small grains added in the intersections of the circles (fig. 102). These are the ornamental loops to the chain of which the flexible part of the bracelet will be made. Take a mandrel of flattened iron or brass wire, coil a strip of thin paper round it, and

165

after the paper flattened or half-round wire, gauge 18 or 20. Saw these links off, and with them loop the first made links in

groups of three and solder each link; the three central ornamental links can be looped together also (fig. 103). You will now be able to loop up the whole 6½ inch length easily, or you can make the bracelet with a single row of ringed loops, as shown in fig. 104. This

FIG. 103.

done, make the two end panels, one to hold the snap and the other for the catch-plate. You can do them in repoussé out of 8-gauge silver. A pair of little rabbits, or squirrels in a bower of leaves, would look well, and the relief should be fairly high. The group should be

FIG. 104.

done in one piece, leaving a clear line down the centre for the joint. When the modelling is complete, boil it out and

166

solder on a back of No. 6 metal. Saw
the panel in two, and solder the slotted
catch-plate centrally on one and the snap-
plate to the other. File out a slot in the
catch-plate side and fit the two together,
and file up clean. When the
thumbpiece has been added, the
clasp is complete, except for
the loops.

Mark on each half the proper
position for the loops of the
chain-band; solder on stout
links of wire. These should
be circles and soldered firmly to
the back-plate of the clasp, and

FIG. 105.

each loop further strengthened by soldering
a grain of silver on each side of it (see
fig. 105). Now loop it all up together,
boil it out, and clean in pickle. Then remove the traces of pickle by boiling it in
hot water and soda. Polish it on the
scratch-brush with beer, and brighten the
domes of each loop with a burnisher. The
clasp can also be gone over with the burnisher with great advantage. It may be
well to mention that springs of catches
made in 9-carat gold last longer than
those made in silver.

167

CHAPTER XIX

Gold Work GOLD work, on account of the greater cost of the material, needs very much more care on the part of the workman. Board sweep, lemel, polishings, the sweepings of the floor underneath the work-bench —must all be carefully preserved for refining when a sufficient quantity has been obtained. The material should always be used, so that it gives its utmost decorative value. The work must be built up out of thin sheets or wires, not filed up out of the solid. Gold, by its very ductility and malleability, invites this method of treatment; and it is the one most used in all the finest periods. To work in solid gold is to waste precious material needlessly. Used thin it gives a beauty unattainable by other means. The quality of the gold to be used depends on the nature of the work. For enamelled panels fine gold is best, but on account of its ex- treme softness it will not stand much wear.

To give it hardness, it is alloyed with varying quantities of copper and silver. Copper by itself gives the gold a red colour, silver by itself a greenish colour; the two together gives the alloy almost the original colour again. The best alloy, both for working and appearance afterwards, is naturally that which is most nearly fine gold—viz., 22-carat. The next best is 20-carat, while the ordinary gold of trade jewellery is 18-carat. But this, if alloyed with copper only, is not pleasant in colour, is much harder to work, and is liable to crack if used for repoussé work. If it is alloyed with silver only the alloy is paler in colour than gold, but it is very pleasant to work, and is very ductile and kindly. For repoussé gold may be alloyed with silver down to 12-carat; but beyond 12-carat the alloy looks much more like silver than gold, and the effect of it is not, perhaps, much better than gold-washed silver. Yet it is as well to remember that the addition of even a small quantity of gold to silver gives a richness of colour which cannot be obtained in any other way.

We will suppose you wish to make a pair of hair ornaments in 20-carat gold. First you will buy from any of the bullion merchants 1 oz. of fine gold. Take 10 dwts. of this, *i.e.* one-half, and to every dwt. add two grains of fine silver and two of alloy copper, in all 1 dwt. 16 grs. Put it in a crucible with a little borax, melt and cast it in a narrow ingot. When cool, draw it out on the anvil into a square wire, hammer the tip taper, and after annealing draw it down with the draw-plate until you get it to size o. Coil it up and anneal it carefully on the mop; boil it out in hydrochloric pickle. Next run the ends into beads, some large for leaves, and some small for berries, and snip off short lengths. You will

FIG. 106.

now need solder.　Take two or three dwts.
of the alloy you are using; to every dwt.
add 5 grains of fine silver, and melt on
the charcoal block with a little borax;

flatten the resulting button of
alloy with a hammer, roll it
out thin, and cut it up into
tiny panels ready for soldering.

FIG. 107.

Take the prepared bits of wire,
flatten the larger beaded ends into leaf
shape with a few taps on the square bench
stake (see fig. 52), group them on either
side of a central stem (see fig. 107), lay
tiny panels of solder over each junction,
and direct the flame on each joint in succession till the whole has been soldered.
Do this until you have as many groups
as you want. In
like manner make
groups of the
smaller beads (fig.
109). Now dome
up a piece of sheet-
iron into a half
ball the size of the

FIG. 108.

proposed ornament. Make two rings of
plain wire, a size or two larger than that
used for the twigs and leaves, and between
them solder a ring of twist wire. This

171

Gold Work is for the foundation band round the edge. This circular band must be soldered to a circle of flattened wire, the wire being bent edgewise. You will next dome up a ball of gold in two halves out of size 1 or 2; when the metal just fits the doming-block, take a file and file away the superfluous metal and having made an air-hole in one half solder the two together. Bend up a

 small strip of metal into a tube about $\frac{3}{16}$ inch long, solder this on a $5\frac{1}{16}$ circle of size 2, domed

 slightly; on the top of the tube solder the gold bead. Next coil up six rings of fine twisted wire, just large enough to fit in between the hollow bead and the base, tie

 them all in position with binding-wire, and solder them to the stem, to the hollow bead and the base

FIG. 109.

(see fig. 110). Make grains out of small lengths of wire or bits of scrap gold, and solder a grain in the angle between the ring and the bead and in the angle between the ring and the base.[1] Round the edge of the base put a double row of twisted wire to enclose the upright rings. Between each pair of rings you must now solder a group of

[1] To solder grains: flush a paillion of solder on back of grain, then borax it, and lay it in place and flame it. The solder will fix grain without appearing on surface.

three grains, but take care not to use too
much heat, or you will melt the rings.
This when boiled out clean, forms the
central boss of the whole ornament. Tie
this and the large ring already made on
the iron ball with binding-wire. You can
now arrange the groups of leaves and
berries in their places between the boss
and the ring. Each group must touch
two others and the top and bottom rings.
If this is not done, the work will not be

strong. While soldering
these it may be well to
paint the parts not to be
soldered with a paste of
loam or whiting and water,
or pipeclay and water, as
a precaution against melting. The solder itself

FIG. 110.

should run more easily than that used for
the groups of leaves. To secure this, take
as much of the first solder as you think
you may require, and add to it a piece
of silver solder, about two grains of silver
solder to each pennyweight of the original
solder. When the soldering is complete,
boil the work clean. Have ready a number of small grains also boiled clean, and
solder one in the angle between the twigs
and the bottom, using this both for

173

appearance and strength (fig. 111). This done, again boil out clean, and having made three circles of wire, size 22, solder them together as in fig. 112. Take a short length of tube, like that you made for the central boss, and tap it with a female screw; file up the ends true and solder it to the centre of the three rings. Fig. 113 shows another arrangement for the bottom of the filagree dome. This trefoil must now be soldered to the back of the bottom ring, and the first part of the work is complete. Fig. 114 shows the knop complete, but with a boss of coiled twist-wire in the centre instead of that first described.

FIG. 111.

The next is to make the pin for attachment to the hair. It should be of 9-carat gold. Take

FIG. 112.

in the proportion of 9 of gold to $7\frac{1}{2}$ of copper and $7\frac{1}{2}$ of silver, i.e. $7\frac{1}{2}$ grains each of copper and silver to 9

174

grains of fine gold will make 1 dwt. of Gold Work
9-carat gold alloy. Having weighed out
your alloy, melted it, and cast the ingot,
draw the ingot out into wire, size 18. Cut
off a piece double the length of the
pin, bend it in the centre, and solder
a segment of wire to make a complete
circle (see fig. 106). This strengthens
the end of the pin. Next make a hinge
out of a small tube
as described for the
brooch hinge (see
fig. 74). On the
centre portion of the
joint solder a male
screw to fit the
female already pre-
pared (see fig. 114.)
File away all rough-
ness; no project-

FIG. 113.

ing points must be left, or they will catch
in the hair and cause inconvenience. All
work intended for wear should be smooth
and pleasant to the touch. The work can
now be stoned and polished with pumice,
crocus, and rouge.

In all jewellery work, but most of all
in gold work, the effect must be built out
of small details. Design is the language

175

Gold Work you learn from your work, and as your skill in handiwork grows, so will your power of design. Design cannot be separated from handiwork. It is the expression of your personality in terms of the material in which you work. One has only to look at any piece of early gold work, Egyptian, Mykenean, Etruscan, Indian, or Anglo-Saxon, to realise what rich effects can be produced by repetition. The beautiful patterns evolved by Arab, Persian, and Hindoo artists from the simplest elements, offer a world of suggestion to the young craftsman, and open up ideas for future use. Do not attempt to copy such work, but study the principles of contrasted line, texture, and form. A grasp of the method of building up all work out of thin sheet, will help you to apply these principles for yourself.

FIG. 114.

176

CHAPTER XX

Gold Necklace with Pendant Fleur de Lys—The Brass Mould—Burnishing the Gold over the Matrix—Another Method of Making Fleur de Lys—Engraved Matrices.

TAKE a piece of brass large enough and thick enough for the pendant, and having carefully transferred to it the outline of your pattern, pierce out the shape with the saw, and file it up to the shape of the pendant (fig. 115), omitting of course the rings and loops for suspension. Take a cement stick (fig. 116), which is merely a short taper handle of wood with roughened end. A good-sized lump of engravers' cement is warmed in the flame of the blow-pipe or spirit lamp and fixed on the roughened end of the stick; the cement while warm is pressed into any shape required by rolling it on a cold iron plate

FIG. 115.

To make engravers' cement:—melt Burgundy pitch, 4 parts; Resin, 4 parts; Plaster of Paris, 2 parts; Beeswax, 2 parts, in a pipkin. Stir well till thoroughly incorporated.

M   177

sprinkled with water to prevent the
cement from sticking. In this case you
will press the warmed cement on the iron so
that you get a level top (fig. 116). Take
the brass model, warm it, and press it into
the cement so that ex-
actly half remains ex-
posed. Smooth the
cement down round the
edges with a wetted steel
spatula. Cool it in water,
and when cold take a
piece of 22 gold, size 2,
anneal it well, and with
a rounded burnisher press
and rub the gold over
the brass shape. Anneal
the gold frequently at
first, and you will find
the work easier. When
you have got the shape
very nearly, warm the
gold, and press it firmly
on the cement until it sticks (fig. 117).
Now with the point of the burnisher
you can drive the gold into the angles,
and finish the shape completely. Remove the brass mould from the cement,
clean it well, and refix it with its other

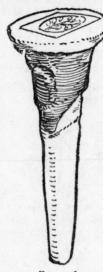

FIG. 116.

178

face upwards. Repeat the burnishing process with another piece of gold, cut away the surplus metal from the outside with the shears, and file up the edges until the two fit perfectly together (see fig. 115), and boil them out. You will

FIG. 117.

now need to strengthen the two halves of the ornament, so that they may not get crushed out of shape after being fastened together. Take snippings of silver or short lengths of silver wire curved to fit the hollows at the back of each half, and

179

solder them in place with panels of
18-carat solder, made by adding 6 grains
of fine silver to every dwt. of fine gold,
or, if you use the scraps and filings from
the 22-carat, 4 grains of fine silver to each
dwt. of scrap. This done, boil the work
clean, tie the two halves together with
fine binding-wire, fitting the edges very
closely to each other or the solder will not
flush properly. Remember that in gold
work you cannot fit too closely ; in silver
work, on the contrary, if the work fits too
well, the solder runs along the surface
and not into the join. When all the joins
are soldered the work can be filed up and
the hanging rings fixed. The smaller
sizes will be made in like manner. If you
wish for more elaborate forms you can
model the shape in wax, and having made
a plaster matrix, make a cast in type-
metal. You can now rub the gold over
the type-metal cast in the same way as
over the brass model ; or, having made
the plaster matrix, you can take a zinc
cast of it in a sand mould, and rub the
gold into it instead of over it. Any irregularities in the mould can be removed
by chasing the surface with repoussé
tools.

Another method is to take a thick piece of brass large enough for your purpose, and having hammered the surface carefully to make the metal uniformly dense and tough, take a scorper, and with it hollow out a matrix of the form you require. The surface of the ornament can be further modelled up with rounded chasing tools to almost any degree of fineness. The effect of your work can be seen by oiling the metal and taking frequent impressions in wax or modelling paste. Into this mould the thin sheet gold can either be rubbed or beaten in with a hammer and a strip of lead (see fig. 118). The lead prevents injury either to the mould or the metal, and by spreading out under the blow, forces the gold into all parts of the mould. If fine silver is used it can with care be hammered solid into the mould, and then filed off true.

Gold Necklace with Pendant

In all these methods it is well to remember that the forms must be clear, and studied closely from nature, or based on some form which you have found by experience looks well in work.

There must be no undercutting or the work will not draw from the mould when you have beaten it in.

The plan of engraving matrices in brass
was one extensively used in old work.
Many of the elaborate necklaces shown
in the Gold Room of the British Museum
are made up of simple forms produced in
moulds like those just described, then

FIG. 118.

soldered together, and linked up with
rough pearls and uncut stones. Having
by one or other of the above methods
made your pendants, group them round
the $4\frac{1}{2}$ circle, and at the points of suspension put either a stone, a simple boss
of gold, or a beehive coil of twisted wire,
182

with a network or open work of wire round it. Solder three strong loops to the backs of these bosses, make some lengths of chain and a snap, and loop the whole together as before.

The central pendant may be made longer, and the side ones hung in diminishing lengths from the centre. For this, make small half balls of thin gold, solder backs to them, and put a ring of twist round the join. Fix two loops opposite to each other on the backs. These will now be linked up between the pendants and the main bosses, completing the necklace.

CHAPTER XXI

Locket or Pendant Casket—The Frame—The Bezel —The Hinge—The Back—Fitting the Hinge— The Joint Tool—Swivel Loops.

THE student would be well advised to attempt this first of all in silver, as these lockets are by no means easy to make. The fitting and the hanging require very great care. Take a piece of silver, size 8, a little wider than the full depth of the pendant (fig. 119). Bend it up into

183

the shape of the outline in fig. 120, and
solder the two ends firmly together. Next
take two plates of size 6, one for the
back and one for the front, dome slightly,
and solder them to the outline frame.
File the surplus metal from the edges and
mark the centre line down the sides of the

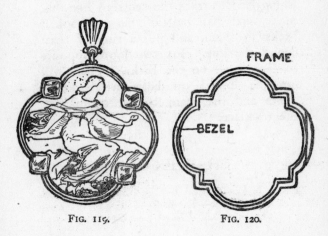

FRAME

BEZEL

FIG. 119.   FIG. 120.

frame, and saw the box apart lengthwise
(fig. 121A). You have now two halves
which exactly fit each other. Mark the
sides, which should come together so that
you may readily fit the two in the right
place. Next take a strip of No. 5, a little
deeper than the sides of each half locket,

184

bend it to fit exactly within the locket, and
solder it in place (fig. 121B). This is to
form the bezel on which the lid
fits, and by which the lid is held
firmly in place. Now boil the
work clean and fit the two together. Having drawn a short
length of small tube from which
to make the hinge, with a small
round file or a joint file make a
deep groove along the line of the
joint (fig. 122). It should be as
deep as possible, so that the tube
may not project and spoil the out- FIG. 121A
line of the pendant. Cut off three lengths
of the tube, so that the three together
just fill the space provided for the hinge.
File the ends of these short lengths true and
square in the joint-tool (fig. 120). Mark

FIG. 121B.

the position of the centre one, and after
taking apart the two halves of the locket,
solder the centre length of tube in its
place on one half of the locket and the
other two lengths on their half. The

185

loop can now be soldered on. It can
be either a plain or a swivel loop.

A swivel loop is made as already described in the chapter on Pendants, only
instead of having the small rings at the
bottom a hole is drilled up through the
point of the loop and a wire, beaded at one

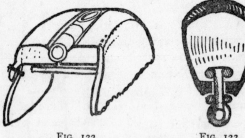

FIG. 122.   FIG. 123.

end, is slipped in, and bent over to form
a ring below the loop (fig. 123). This
ring should be soldered. The swivel and
the hole must be painted with a little
rouge and water, so that the solder may
not run and make a solid instead of a
swivel joint. Stones may be set on the
front and the front panel cut away, leaving a narrow rim. An enamel panel can
then be fixed in from the back, as described in the chapter on Settings.

186

CHAPTER XXII

Carving in Metal—Where Carving is Necessary—
Making the Tools—Tempering—The Wax
Model—The Use of the Chisels—Finishing
—The Spiral Knop—The Wreathed Setting.

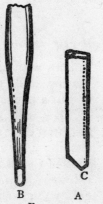

FIG. 124.

SMALL figures, wreaths, sprays, and small animals and birds, can be very easily carved out of the solid metal. As mentioned in another chapter, where the work is to be enamelled, it is necessary that it should be carved out of a material which is perfectly even in texture or the enamel will fly off. The tools required are exceedingly simple. A few chisels of various sizes made out of short lengths of bar steel, a chasing-hammer, and a few files and ordinary repoussé tools will alone be necessary.

To Make the Tools.—Cut off a few 5-inch lengths of square bar steel of different sizes and different widths; soften the ends by heating them to a cherry red. Let them cool gradually. File the ends

187

of each into a blunt bevel (see fig. 124, A, B). Fig. 125 shows an enlarged view of the cutting end of the tool. Fix each in the vice and file off the square edges along

FIG. 125.

the sides and the top, so that the tool will be more comfortable to the hand. It will be well to have one or two made with a rounded bevel like a gouge, and one with a rather sharp bevelled edge for occasional use. Having got them filed up into shape, and the sides and top made nice and smooth with emery-cloth, harden each by heating it to a cherry red and dropping it into a bucket of cold water.

They will now need tempering. First brighten the metal at the cutting edge by rubbing it on emery-cloth. Then hold the tool in the flame until the first pale straw colour comes. Have ready a vessel of cold water, and as soon as the colour appears, cool the tool in the water. When all have been treated, you will be ready to begin to work.

Take your lump of silver or gold, hammer it well all over to make it more

188

dense and uniform in texture. It is well
to have the metal longer than the object
you wish to carve, so that you can hold
it in a small bench-vice while carving.

Before beginning, it is wise to take the
precaution of making a model in wax of
the subject you intend to carve. Block
out the principal masses with the gouge-
shaped chisel. Do not be too eager to
get down to the surface of your model.
It is better to get the action and movement before attempting modelling in detail. Then, with the smaller chisels you
can go over the work, and realise the form
more completely, taking care always to
drive the chisel along the line of the bevel
which rests upon the work (see fig. 124, C).
At this stage you may take the work out
of the vice and put it on the pitch-block,
and work it up with repoussé tools. Oval
matting-tools, with a slightly rounded
surface, will be found very useful for this.
Use the chisels now and then to remove
any metal which by repeated working has
become too hard to yield to the tracing-tool.
With smooth punches and tracers you can
get almost any degree of fineness of work.
If, however, the work is to be afterwards
enamelled, it is useless to spend too much

time upon surface modelling ; a great deal
must be left to be done in the enamelling.

Sprays of leaves and flowers or knops
of leafage can be very easily produced
by this method in the following manner.
Suppose you wish to carve a spiral knop
of nut leaves.
Take a piece of
16-gauge silver,
beat it into a
dome of the size
and depth of your
knop. Anneal
the metal. Now
draw with a fine
brush and Indian
ink the spiral
twigs and the
masses of leaves.
See that branches

FIG. 126.

or twigs stretch from each line of the spiral
to the lines above and below it (fig. 126).
This is in order that the knop may be strong
all over. With a drill and a fret-saw pierce
out the interspaces. Take your gravers,
begin with the round scorper, after wetting
the tip of the tool, and cut grooves lengthwise along the twigs, so that the spiral
growth of the twig is emphasised. Next,

190

with a flat scorper cut the groups of leaves
so as to show their overlapping. With
a small gouge you can now vein the leaves
and add any necessary finishing touches to
the twigs. The knop may be finished up
still further by putting it upon the pitch
and adding any refinements of detail you
may desire.

How to Carve a Wreathed Setting.—A
fine stone will
often look well
in a conical
wreathed setting
carved out of
thick sheet metal
(fig. 127). Mark
out the section

FIG. 127.

of the setting at A, fig. 128. Produce
the sides till they meet. From this point
as centre draw circles as shown. On the
base make a semicircle, and divide it into
any number of equal parts, say 16. Set
out these on the larger segment, join the
last point to the centre. The enclosed
form is that required to make the setting.
Cut this shape out with the shears,
bend the metal up to fit the stone, and
solder the edges. Draw on this (fig. 129)
a wavy spiral of twigs, and while keeping

191

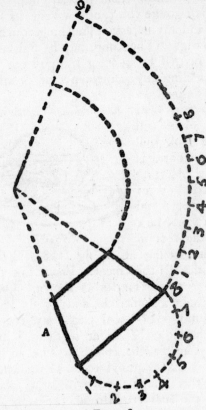

FIG. 128.

branches and leaves are well knit together.
192

Pierce out the interspaces with the drill and saw. Then take an engraving-stick and a piece of gold-beater's skin, warm the cement on the stick, and shape it with a wetted thumb and forefinger just to fit the setting. Place the skin over the warmed cement, and press the set-ting, also warmed, well down upon the skin-covered surface. The

FIG. 129.

cement will press the skin out through the holes in the setting, and when cold will keep it firmly in its place. Unless the skin is used the cement is apt to spread all over the metal, so that you cannot see what you are doing. You can now carve the work with scorpers, as before described.

CHAPTER XXIII

Casting — The Cuttlefish Mould—Flasks—The Loam—Smoking the Mould—Slate or Bath-brick Moulds.

VERY small castings, such as reliefs to set in rings and sprays of foliage, heads, birds,

N 193

&c., can very easily be done in cuttlefish bone. Choose a clean and perfect specimen cuttlefish, cut it in half, and rub each face perfectly flat. Insert three small register pegs in one face (fig. 130), leaving plenty of room between for the pattern. Press the two faces together, so that they

FIG. 130.

fit absolutely close. Lay the pattern, which must not be anywhere undercut, in the space between the pegs, and press the two halves of the mould carefully and firmly, so that you may get a perfectly clear impression. Take them apart, re-

194

move the pattern, make a funnel-shaped channel for the metal, also channels for air-holes, leading radially outwards (fig. 131), and tie the mould up with binding-

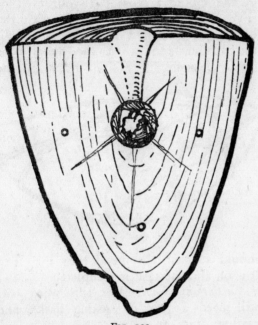

FIG. 131.

wire (fig. 132). Make a little pit in a piece of charcoal large enough to take the gold or silver you wish to melt, tie

195

the charcoal to the top of the mould, so that the pit comes opposite the channel or " pour." Make another channel from the hollow in the charcoal to the channel in the mould. Now put your gold or silver in the charcoal, melt it with the blow-pipe, adding a little borax to aid the fusion, and when the metal runs into a clear shining molten globe, tilt the

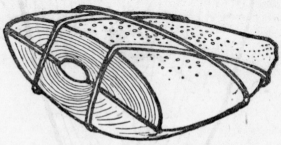

Fig. 132.

mould so that the metal runs in. Let it cool, and the task is complete.

Casting in Sand.—For this work you will need a pair of casting flasks, fine casting sand or loam, some black lead and French chalk in powder, and a muslin bag full of pea-flour to dust over the patterns and the surfaces of the mould. Casting flasks are two equal-sized frames

196

of cast-iron, one of which has flanges carrying pegs which fit into holes in corresponding flanges on the other frame. The first is called the peg side, the second the eye side. Lay the eye side flange downwards on a perfectly flat, smooth board. Within this, rather near to the funnel-shaped entrance to the flask, the pattern will afterwards be laid. We will suppose it to be a piece of relief work with a flat back. It should be well rubbed over with black lead, so that the sand may not stick to it.

Now take some handfuls of the moulding sand and loam, wet the mixture with water sprinkled over it, just enough being used to make the loam bind. When you have mixed loam and sand thoroughly, press it down and beat it well into the mould with a mallet. Strike the upper surface level with a straight-edge, and, having placed a bit of board upon the mould, turn it over eye side upwards. Dust the surface of the mould with finely powdered brick-dust. This is to prevent the two surfaces of the mould from sticking together. Lay the pattern, which must be well brushed over with black lead, upon the surface of the mould on the centre line, but not too near

197

the opening into the mould. If the pattern is placed too near the opening the weight of metal above the pattern will not be sufficient when it is being poured in to force the liquid metal into all the crevices of the matrix. On the other hand, it must not be too far away or it may take more metal than you happen to have at your disposal. Take the pattern, press it half-way into the mould, dust the whole surface of the pattern and the mould with fine brick-dust. Now place the peg side in position, press the loam very carefully in by hand, and then beat it well in with the mallet. Take the peg side off, blow away loose particles of sand from each side, and very carefully remove the pattern. The mould must now be dusted with powdered charcoal or pea-flour, or smoked with a burning taper, and the pattern once more placed in position, the two halves pressed firmly together, so as to take the final impression of the pattern. Loosen the sand over the pattern with a knife, and then drive it home again with repeated blows with the mallet. Remove the pattern, make the pour and a few air-channels leading away from any prominent part of the pattern, so that the air can escape when driven out by the inrush of the molten metal. The moulds should now be put over a gas-burner to dry, which must be done very thoroughly. When it is quite dry melt your metal in a good-sized crucible, and while the mould is warm pour the metal quickly in. The casting when cool can be filed up and chased as much as you wish.

The methods just described are only useful for comparatively rough work to be afterwards chased. When a fine surfaced cast is required, or when there is much detail in the model, the moulds must be made as described in chapters xxxi. and xxxii.

Moulds for simple objects may be made of slate, steatite, or bath-brick. The forms desired can very easily be hollowed out of any of these materials. Bath-brick, however, will only serve for a few casts, while the others will last for a long time. There are several interesting specimens of these moulds, with examples of the work produced by them, in the Mediæval Room of the British Museum.

CHAPTER XXIV

**Enamel
Work**

THE use of enamel in jewellery is to add
richness and colour. It should not be
used in large masses or the effect will
be heavy, and the most valuable quality
of enamel, which is preciousness, will be
lost. The colours used should be pure
and brilliant and few in number. As a
general rule each colour should be separated from its neighbour by a line of metal,
and be also bordered by a line of metal.
That is to say, where the enamel is used
to decorate a surface it should be enclosed
in cells, made either by cutting them out
of the surface with gravers and scorpers,
or by raising the walls of the cells from
the back, or by soldering flattened wire
bent to shape edgewise to form the cell
walls or cloisons: the cloisons form a
kind of network which encloses the enamel
in its meshes and carries the metal con-

200

struction through the design. The colour
and sheen of the metal outline harmonise
the different colours with each other, and
give a greater brilliancy of effect than can
be obtained by any other means. The
colour of the metal, in fact, is a valuable
ground tint. The limitations of this
method are great, but in those very limitations lies the strength of the student.
The scheme must be completely thought
out, the outline must be clear, and the
colour clean and pure. Nothing can be
left to chance. Many valuable hints can
be gained by a careful study of Indian
enamel work ; that of Jeypore in particular is full of suggestiveness and beauty.
Enamel may be used as a background for
set stones, or an effect of colour made the
motive of a design, but in all cases care
should be taken to secure a clear metal
outline.

For translucent enamel pictures the metal
outline cannot of course be used ; but in
this case the whole picture should be small
enough to set as a jewel. The burnished
edge of the setting then takes the place of
the metal outline.

Large plaques of enamel are unsuitable
for personal ornament. If enamel is to be

201

used on small figure subjects, the figures should either be beaten up in the round from sheet, or carved out of solid metal. Enamel rarely stands on cast work, partly because of the inequality of texture of the metal, and partly because the metal is so full of minute air-holes. It will hold for a time, especially if soft; but sooner or later will fly off in the form of tiny flakes. This can in some measure be prevented by stabbing the ground of the enamel with a sharp graver, so that little points of metal are left sticking up all over the surface. These hold the enamel fairly well, but you can never be sure that it will not flake off just where it will most be seen. The best grounds for enamel are fine alloy copper, fine silver, fine gold, and 22-carat gold.

The various methods of enamelling will probably be familiar to most students, through Mr. Cunynghame's recent work on the subject. It will therefore be unnecessary to do more than to treat each process briefly, and refer those who may desire fuller information to that work.

Requisites.—The following things will be found useful :—

A china mortar and pestle.

A small agate mortar and pestle.

A nest of covered palettes as used for water-colours.

A slab of ground glass about 12 inches square.

A large rounded hæmatite burnisher.

A few wide-mouthed glass bottles with corks, to hold the enamels.

A few pieces of sheet - iron. Some binding-wire.

A corundum file.

A small flask of hydrofluoric acid. A 6-inch dipping-tube, made of ¼-inch tube, to use with this acid. A lead trough made by bending up the sides of a square of rolled sheet-lead — that at 5 lbs. to the foot will do.

A good strong painter's palette-knife.

A long-handled pair of tongs.

A muffle-furnace, or, for small work, a crucible.

Cloisonné—How to make a Brooch in Cloisonné Enamel.—Take a piece of 22-carat gold, size 4, the size of a shilling, and with a good-sized burnisher rub it into a very flat dome. Draw a piece of gold-wire through an oblong-holed draw-plate until it is about size 10. Bend it into a ring a little smaller than the disc. Solder the ends

203

of the wire together in the flame with
18-carat solder. Make both disc and ring
clean, and solder the ring so that it makes
a rim to the plate. Have ready some
flattened gold wire, drawn several sizes
smaller than the first, and having decided
on your design, bend the wire edgewise
into the shape required; dip it into borax
water, and place it in position. Get a
section of the design done in this way,
then charge the work with snippets of
18-carat solder and tack the wires in their
places. It is not necessary to flush the
joints fully. Boil the work out and
proceed until the panel is complete (fig.
133).

Some enamellers do not solder the
cloisons; but if they are not soldered,
when the enamel is fired again the cloisons
may float about and get out of place. Still,
if the gold back is thick, and a few of the
main cloisons and the outer ring are soldered, the remainder can well be left to
be fixed by the melting of the enamel.

Now, having chosen your enamel, suppose opal for the ground, green for the
leaves, blue for the dividing rays; grind
up each colour separately in the small
agate mortar, and when it is like fine sand,

FIG. 133.

mel by pouring clean water over it until

the residue is clear, sparkling, and crystalline. Now, with a small spatula fill each cell or cloison with the proper colour, taking care that no grains of colour get into neighbouring cells. Drain away the superfluous water with bits of clean blotting-paper, fill the other cells, and dry them in like manner. You will now make a support out of a square of thin sheet-iron, having the centre bossed up to fit the underside of the brooch. Paint this over with loam or whitening and water with a very little borax added. When it is dry, place the work upon the support, and having dried the enamel on an iron plate heated by a spirit lamp or a bunsen burner, place it in the muffle for about a minute until the enamel fuses. Take it out, and boil in dilute acid to remove the dark scale of oxide which has formed on the surface. You will find that the enamel on fusing has greatly shrunk in volume; refill the cells with the same enamels as before and refire, repeating the process until the cells are full. When this happens, smooth the whole surface with a corundum file and water, wash the grit away with a little hydrofluoric acid and water (use indiarubber finger-stalls for this work, and

take care not to get any of the acid on
your flesh). You can now fire the work
again, just enough to glaze the surface,
and after pickling away the scale of oxide.
polish it with putty on a soft buff. Make
a frame and a setting for it out of 20 or
22-carat gold—the frame would be a piece
of flat wire or a strip of No. 7 gauge bent
round flatwise into a flat ring and soldered.
On this you will fix the thin band, size
No. 3 or 4, to fit the enamel panel. In
the angle between the edge of the flat ring
and the upright face of the setting you
may solder a row of small grains alternately with lengths of plain wire thus

···· ——···· ——   o——··o··——··o··——o

or double rows of right and left hand twist
in short lengths, with small half-domes
of thin gold soldered on at intervals. The
catch and joint can now be made of 18-
carat gold, and a pin out of 9-carat gold.
When the frame and pin have been polished,
the enamel centre can be set and the edge
burnished over evenly all round.

It is quite possible to solder the ring
which takes the joint and catch on the
back of the brooch before the cloisons are
soldered on. The joints and the soldered

207

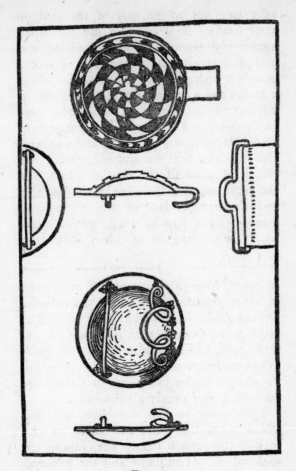

FIG. 134.

rim are protected from the heat by whitening or loam; the whole thing is then put in the furnace. Great care, however, is needed lest the joint or catch should drop off in the muffle. The latter way is the simpler looking, and the possibility of an imperfect setting is avoided. The brooch can also be made in fine silver, but if the last-named method is used for the catch it must be soldered with 18-carat gold solder; silver solder eats holes in the metal when heated in the muffle.

Champlevè Enamel—How to Make a Buckle in Enamel.—Take a piece of fine silver, size 15, and mark out upon it the size of the buckle. Dome the centre slightly, and make a flattened border round the dome (fig. 134). The pattern you devise had better be a simple one for the first attempt. That given above you will probably find fairly simple to cut and yet elaborate enough to give you plenty of opportunity for arrangements of colour. Before setting to work on the silver it will be well to make one or two trials on copper. Fix the metal either on an engraver's block with cement or on an ordinary pitch-block, or, if the work be small enough, on an engraving stick.

Have ready a few scorpers of different sizes and shapes (see figs. 135, 136), flat, half-round, and pointed, and a good oil-stone. Hold the scorper blade between the thumb and forefinger, and the handle in the hollow of the palm. The point

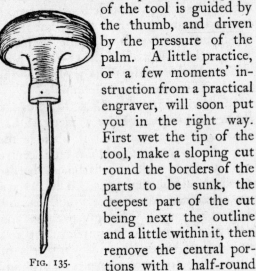

of the tool is guided by the thumb, and driven by the pressure of the palm. A little practice, or a few moments' instruction from a practical engraver, will soon put you in the right way. First wet the tip of the tool, make a sloping cut round the borders of the parts to be sunk, the deepest part of the cut being next the outline and a little within it, then remove the central portions with a half-round

FIG. 135.

scorper; then take a straight scorper, and go all over the ground with a rocking side-to-side motion of the tool, making a zig-zag cut thus $\lessgtr$. This roughens the ground, and makes the enamel hold better than on a smooth surface. If translucent enamels are used, however, this surface has a mechanical look which is rather objectionable, and if the sides of each cell are slightly undercut the enamel will hold quite well. When you have

FIG. 136.

got the whole pattern cleanly cut you can now fix the bars which are to carry the belt, and solder them firmly with 18-carat gold solder, or with a specially hard alloy of silver and copper composed of—

211

	oz.	dwt.	grs.
Fine silver	1	0	0
Fine copper	0	5	0
	1	5	0

If the latter is used the soldered portions must be carefully protected from the heat of the furnace by loam and whitening or plaster of Paris and borax. When the soldering is done you must go over the work again with a flat scorper, and remove the white skin or " boil" produced by the pickle. If this is not done the enamel will not hold.

The next thing is the enamelling. The best colours for silver are blues, greens, purples, and opal. A good scheme for this buckle would be deep but not dark blue, rich apple-green, and opal and dark green in the outer border. Grind the enamels as before described, but not too finely. The coarser you can use the enamel the better the colour; wash each clear of milkiness, and fill every cell with its proper colour; dry the work, and fire in the muffle on a cradle of sheet-iron made to fit the back of the buckle, or in a crucible with a cover, using a blow-pipe and foot-bellows. Greater brilliancy can be

212

obtained by using clear flux as the first layer, and adding the colours only after the first firing ; or in some of the cells a ground of flux can be laid, and bits of gold foil, pricked full of holes (with a bunch of fine needles set in a cork), can be laid on the flux, covered over first with a thin layer of flux and then with a thin layer of green or a fine red. The cells will need refilling and refiring until they are full. The surface can now be filed smooth with a corundum file, washed in hydrofluoric and water, refired, and the whole afterwards polished with rouge.

How to Make a Pendant in Limoges Enamels.—Take a piece of thin Swedish or French copper of the size required. With a burnisher rub it into a slight dome shape, and turn up the edge very slightly all round by burnishing it over the edge of a round-paned hammer fixed in a vice. Next pickle it in dilute nitric acid until the metal is perfectly clean. Paint the back of the plate with gum tragacanth and water, and sprinkle the dry waste enamel which results from the washings over the back from a pepper-pot or tea-strainer ; shake off the superfluous enamel, and let it dry. Now take the colour you

213

have selected for the foundation, grind it and wash clean, put it in a china-colour saucer, mix a tiny drop of tragacanth with the enamel, and dab it over the face of the plaque with a brush. When the whole surface is evenly covered, take away any superfluous moisture with a bit of blotting-paper or a piece of clean, dry, old linen rag. Press the enamel down evenly and smoothly all over with a stiff palette-knife. Have ready an iron cradle or support domed to fit the underside of the plaque, and painted with loam or whitening as before described; dry the enamel over the spirit lamp, and fire in the muffle or in the crucible until the surface is smooth enough to reflect the palette-knife when held over it. Take it out, let it cool slowly, and when cold repair any faults in the surface by cleaning the metal in pickle and by rubbing down with a corundum file. Wash the surface clean, repair the holes with fresh enamel, and refire. You will now take some silver foil, prick it all over with the needle, and cut out leaves, as many as you need, and a piece of gold foil large enough for the rose; fix them in their places on the plaque with a little tragacanth, cover each with a thin layer of flux, and fire it. Now cover each leaf thinly with green, and the rose with red enamel. You can get the effect of slight modelling by laying the enamel on the rose thicker at the top of the petals than at the bottom, but it must not be too thick or it will flake off. The spray can now be outlined carefully and firmly with a fine-pointed miniature brush and shell gold. This outline can be fixed by being fired. It must not be fired too much, or the particles of gold will sink into the enamel and the outline disappear. The work can now be set either as a pendant, as a panel in a necklace, or a centre for a buckle or clasp.

How to Make Network Enamels or Plique à Jour.—In this method the enamel when finished has no ground, but is supported by a metal network within the substance of the enamel. Get a flat sheet of aluminium bronze or platinum about 10 gauge, and burnish the surface quite bright. This is to form the temporary ground. Next take a piece of stout silver or gold wire, and bend it into the shape of the enclosing line of this proposed panel.

Next take some cloison wire, which you can buy, or make by drawing round wire through a draw-plate with oblong holes in it, or the wire can be drawn through a square hole and flattened in the rolling-mill.

You can make a draw-plate out of a piece of an old flat file by heating it red hot, and driving a hardened taper steel punch of the right size through the steel. Larger holes can be made by driving the punch in still farther, or the hole can be made smaller by beating the hole down with a rounded hammer, and again driving the punch through to the required distance. Take the wire and bend it up to form the outline of the leaves, or the fish, or whatever pattern you may wish, and solder the outlines together. Take great care to have the whole well tied together (fig. 137). The leaves should touch each other, the stems, and, where possible, the frame. The strength of the work when finished depends on the thoroughness with which this is done. You now have the skeleton design. Boil it out and scrape the sides of the cloisons bright, lay the work on the burnished plate, fill the cells with ground enamel well washed, and fire in a fairly quick heat. Let it cool gradually, fill up the cells where the enamel is deficient, and refire. When all the cells

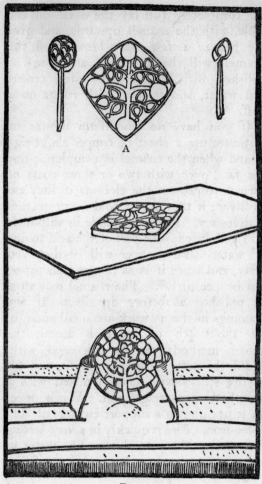

Fig. 137.

are completely full lay the work on the
table, with the enamel upwards, and give
the bronze a few sharp blows, and the
enamel will be released, and can be
polished with emery and water, crocus
and water, and finished with rouge on a
buff.

If you have no aluminium bronze or
platinum use a sheet of copper about size
5, and when the enamel is complete paint
the face over with two or three coats of
varnish to protect the cloisons if they are
of silver; if they are of gold no protection
is necessary. Place the whole in sulphuric
acid and water—one part of the acid to one
of water. The copper will be dissolved
away, and when it is as thin as thin paper,
can be peeled off. The enamel may then
be polished as before described. If the
openings in the network are small enough,
i.e. about ⅛th of an inch across, the
above methods can be dispensed with.
Hold the network panel upright, and fill
in the spaces with enamel mixed with a
very little gum tragacanth. When done,
fix it upright on a support cut out of thin
sheet-iron. Fire it quickly in a very strong
fire, so that the enamel runs like water in
the spaces. It must be cooled carefully,

and not taken away from the heat too
suddenly, or the enamels may crack away
from the cloisons and the effect spoilt.
A panel like fig. 138 would look well
in a skeleton setting, and would do either
for a brooch or a pendant for a necklace.
Another way is to cut out the spaces
with a piercing-saw, leaving the cloisons
slightly thicker, and filing them down
afterwards. This does away with the
need of sol-
der, but it is
more labori-
ous, and the
result lacks
the freedom

FIG. 138.

and life of the methods just described.

How to do an Intaglio or Deep-Cut Enamel.
—In this work the forms are carved or
modelled below the surface of the metal,
at the bottom of a shallow pit, as it were.
The pit is afterwards filled up with enamel,
fired, and then ground and polished level
with the surface of the metal. Where the
carving is deepest the enamel is darkest
in colour, and *vice versa.* Having decided
on your design, suppose a leaf pattern
as at A (fig. 137), take a piece of hardish
modelling-wax and make a model in very

219

low relief. When the outline is clean, and definitely expresses your intention, make a mould from it in the finest plaster of Paris. This will give you a good idea of the depth of your cutting. Copy this in silver or copper—the metal should not be less than 16 gauge, or you will soon cut through to the other side. Fix a piece of the metal, cut nearly to the size and shape you require, on an engraving stick or on a pitch-block, and with a spit-stick outline the design; then cut the design deeply round the edges within this line. Thus, if for a leaf, the cross section of your cutting would be thus ‿‿‿. The stalks would be deep grooves, and the flowers carved to suggest them as nearly as possible. The sides of the sinkings must be kept upright; if they have become irregular, they can be trued up with a justifier, which is a scorper ground with two cutting edges at an angle to each other as in fig. 139. B and C are the cutting edges. When the modelling is as complete as you can make it, and the surface of it everywhere bright, put the enamel in and press

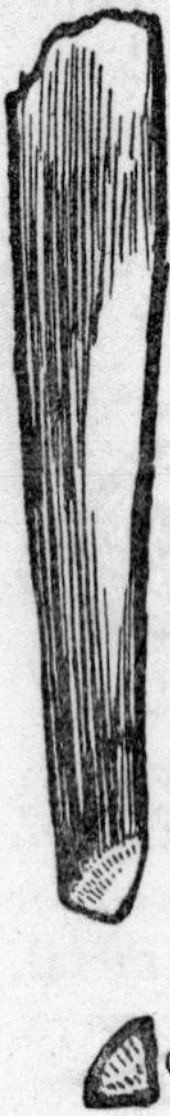

FIG. 139.

it down; when fired, and the enamel filed and polished, the relief is, as it were, translated into a shaded drawing in colour. If you do figure-work, the faces, hands, and feet, can be left in metal and afterwards engraved in line, the backgrounds and draperies alone being deep cut and enamelled. An etcher's dry-point is useful for fine work in the hair and features. The lines of the engraving can be afterwards filled in with etching-ball or thick black paint or shoemaker's heel-ball.

Small figure-panels in raised gold or silver can be produced by first doing the work in ordinary gesso on a piece of smooth, hard wood. Fine silver or fine gold, rolled to the thinness of common notepaper, is then annealed, and burnished over the relief in the same way that a schoolboy makes the foil copies of a shilling. When the metal impression is as complete as the gesso original it can be fixed on the pitch-block, and the modelling carried still farther with pointed burnishers. This, when enamelled back and front, can be set in a frame and fixed in a bracelet or a pendant. Panels for altar-crosses, candlesticks, &c., can be so produced. They can be strengthened

221

by backing with cement composition.
Make the wall of the setting which is
to enclose them ⅛ or ¼ inch deeper than
would be necessary for the enamel itself.
When everything is ready for setting the
enamels, melt some rosin in a pipkin, and
add to it about half its bulk of plaster of
Paris or powdered whitening; stir it well,
pour it into the setting, warm the enamel
slightly, and press it into its place; and
when cold, burnish the edge of the setting
carefully over the enamel and clean it
with methylated spirit and a soft rag.
Almost any composition with a resinous
base which sets hard would, however,
serve the purpose equally well. Figures
in higher relief can be done by taking a
cast in type-metal from a model in wax.
The thin metal is then rubbed and burnished over the type-metal and frequently
annealed during the process. Or the
reverse of the model may be cast in type-
metal or pewter, and the thin gold or
silver rubbed into it. This, of course,
cannot be done if there is any under-
cutting.

222

CHAPTER XXV

Hinges for Casket—Drawing the Tube—The Mandrel—The Liner—The Joint Tool—Soldering the Joints—The Pin.

TAKE a strip of metal, say size 6, thrice wider than the diameter of the proposed hinge. Suppose the hinge to be ⅛th of an inch in diameter, the width of the strip of metal would be ⅜. Mark this off the sheet with the dividers, running one leg of the dividers down the edge as a guide (fig. 140). Snip off the angles at one end of the strip as shown in fig. 141. This is to make the end taper, so that it will slip into the hole in the draw-plate. Now fix in the vice a block of wood one inch wide in which you have made a few graduated semicircular notches (fig. 142), and with the end of the hammer beat the strip of metal into a hollow gutter lengthwise (fig. 143). Bend it still farther round at one end until it is a rough tube-shape (fig. 144), and anneal it in the fire or blow-pipe flame. While it is still hot rub it over inside and out with a little beeswax. Take a steel mandrel, which is a

223

length of polished steel wire, as thick as
the inside of the proposed tube, file the

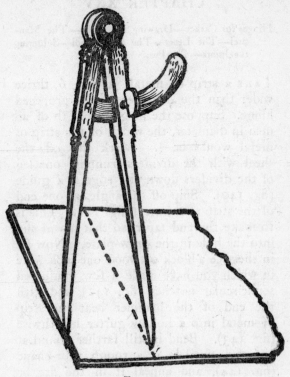

FIG. 140.

end taper (see fig. 145). Place the taper
end in the rough tube, and squeeze the

224

metal round the mandrel at the end (fig.
146). Now fix the draw-plate in the vice,
slip mandrel and tube together through a
suitable hole in the draw-plate, and draw
them by hand through successive holes
until the metal becomes a tube which
nearly fits the mandrel. Now place the
draw-plate on the draw-bench, and draw
the tube and mandrel together until the
latter fits fairly tightly.
Now put the reverse end
of the mandrel into a
hole in the plate which
exactly fits it, and draw
it out either by hand
or with the draw-bench.
The tube is now com-
plete. It can be made
still smaller if necessary
by drawing it through

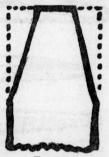

FIG. 141.

the holes in the plate without the mandrel.

In like manner draw another tube a
little larger in diameter, so that the tube
first made will just fit inside. Anneal
both tubes; saw the large tube in two
halves lengthwise, and take two strips of
metal as wide as the edge of the casket
and as long, and solder a half tube to
each (fig. 147). File away the outside

FIG. 142.

FIG. 143.

FIG. 144.

FIG. 145.

FIG. 146.

FIG. 147.

FIG. 148.

quarter of each semicircle (figs. 148 and 149) to allow for the lid to open. Divide the length of the casket into an unequal number of small spaces from $\frac{1}{2}$ inch to 1 inch, according to the greater or less length of

FIG. 149.

the hinge; cut the smaller tube into corresponding lengths, and file the joints flat in the joint-tool (fig. 150). Fit the two halves of the hinge together, and lay the short lengths of tube along the groove close together (fig. 149), and with a small panel of solder tack the alternate lengths to one side of the hinge (see fig. 151), taking care not to run the solder into the joints between the tubes. Take the two halves apart, and soundly solder each length of tube in its place. Do not forget to clean the work in pickle

FIG. 150.

after each soldering. The hinge is now

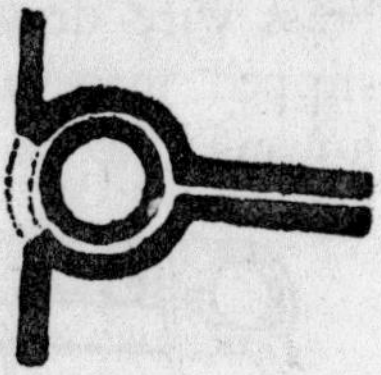

227

ready for the pin, which may be a piece of brass wire drawn to the proper size and slipped into place. The pin must not, however, be fixed until the casket is other-

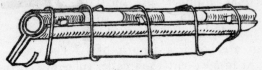

FIG. 151.

wise complete. The work may now be filed up clean, made true, and each half carefully fitted and soldered into its place on the lid of the box.

CHAPTER XXVI

Mouldings—The Swage-Block—Filing the Grooves —Drawing the Metal.

FOR this you will need a swage-block (see fig. 152) with movable dies (see figs. 153 and 154).

In the upper surface of one of the dies file a groove of the shape of the moulding you require as in fig. 153. The groove must be trumpet-shaped, the smaller end being the exact section you wish the

228

moulding to be. This must be done
with great care, as the smallest mark will

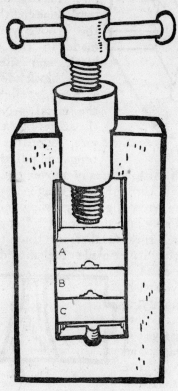

Fig. 152

show on the moulding. Now cut a strip

Mouldings of metal slightly thicker and wider than the proposed mould-

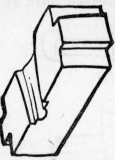

ing. Having annealed it, pass one end through the groove you have made in the swage-block, and screw the plain block down so as to press slightly on the metal. Now fix the swage-block in the vice, take the draw-tongs and pull the strip

Fig. 153.

through with a steady movement. Pass the strip through the swage again and turn the screw slightly, pressing the metal more closely into the mould. Repeat this, annealing the metal from time to time until you have made the moulding as complete and as thin as you wish.

By modifying the section of the groove in the swage, and by filing the lower surface of

Fig. 154.

the upper swage-block, hollow mould-ings of almost any section can be produced, provided, of course, that no part is undercut.

CHAPTER XXVII

THE materials required will be polishing sticks, which are flat strips of wood covered on one side with chamois leather—one for use with oil and pumice and one for rouge and water. A ringstick, a round, tapering, leather-covered rod of wood, will be found useful for polishing the insides of rings. A few mops, scratch-brushes, and a leather buff, together with pumice-stone, rotten-stone, crocus, sticks of charcoal, and a small quantity of jeweller's rouge, will complete what is necessary for most kinds of polishing.

Polishing Silver Work.—Silver work is polished in several ways according to the degree of lustre desired.

For a very brilliant polish the method is as follows :—After the work has been pickled or boiled out clean in dilute acid,

231

the whole visible surface is carefully stoned
over with sticks of Water of Ayr stone,
working with a circular motion to avoid
scratching or grooving the metal. Internal
angles, narrow grooves, and shallow lines,
are stoned with thin slips of slate. The
work must be wiped clean from time to
time to see that the surface is being evenly
polished. The object of stoning is the
removal of the film of oxide produced by
heat, and all marks of the tools and files.
The surface is next more finely polished
with charcoal and oil; you can add a
little crocus to hasten the process if you
wish. This done, polish again with fine
rotten-stone and oil, taking care in each
process to avoid lines, scratches, or marks
of any kind. The final polish is given
with jeweller's rouge and water, and the
work washed in hot soap and water to
remove all traces of grease. This process
is laborious, but the result, when properly
carried out, is most brilliant.

A more rapid method, used for ordinary
work or for polishing repoussé, is as follows :—The work is stoned as before and
then scratch-brushed on the lathe, and
sprinkled from time to time with stale beer.
Mouldings, bosses, ribs, or projections

from the surface can be brightened still
further by burnishing with a smooth burnisher. A little soap and water used with
the tool makes it work more easily. Indian workers simplify the process still
further. The surface of the metal, after
being carefully whitened in pickle, is
scraped over with the scraper, and afterwards vigorously burnished with agate
and hæmatite burnishers; but unless both
scraping and burnishing are most carefully
done, the work, as might be expected,
will look rough and unfinished.

Polishing Gold Work.—The process of
polishing gold work is very similar to that
first described for silver. The work is
boiled out as before and stoned. Then
put a little finely powdered pumice into
a shallow vessel, and mix it into a paste
with olive oil. Take a boxwood polishing-
stick—a skewer or a slip of any hard
wood will do—dip the point in the oil and
pumice, and rub over the whole work,
cleaning out crevices, sunk lines, &c.,
most carefully. If this be not done, the
oxidised surface at the bottom of the
hollows will remain as whitish patches
scattered over the otherwise polished surface with a disfiguring effect. In time

this defect is removed, the hollows get filled with dirt, and the work looks more interesting. It is better not to rely on the result of time; besides the reflected light from the bottom of the hollows when polished often makes the work look richer and more full of colour.

When you have gone over the whole surface with the oil and pumice, the process is continued with oil and crocus, and completed with rouge and water. In the case of both gold and silver work, the polishings and scourings of the metal should always be kept and refined to recover the precious metal which has been removed in the process. The burnishers, mops, and polishing-brushes must all be kept perfectly clean and free from dust. Unless this be done, the work may be scratched and spoilt when most near completion.

The burnishers should be occasionally polished on the buff, and kept wrapped up in chamois leather when not in use.

CHAPTER XXVIII

Colouring, Darkening, or Oxidising Silver and Gold Work—Materials Required—Darkening Gold—Colouring Copper.

SILVER work, when newly whitened and polished, always looks unpleasantly white and glaring. Time will always remedy this, but the process can be hastened. This can be done by oxidising the surface with any of the compounds of sulphur. The work may be exposed to the fumes of sulphur, or it may be washed with solutions of any of the chemical compounds of sulphur, such as potassium sulphide, ammonium sulphide, barium sulphide, &c. The ammonium sulphide is what is most generally used, and it gives a range of colour to polished silver, varying from pale golden straw through deep crimson to purple and bluish black. The depth of the colour depends on the strength of the solution and the length of time the metal is exposed to its action.

The simplest way of applying it is to make a hot solution of the ammonium sulphide—not too strong, a pale straw

235

colour will give about the proper strength. Do this in the open air if possible, as the odour disengaged is most offensive; then brush a little of the solution over the work you desire to darken. Watch closely until you perceive the colour you wish for, then swiftly wash the work in clean water, and dry it. If the surface be now rubbed gently with a chamois leather the film of oxide is removed from the projecting portions of the work, giving it a much richer, older appearance.

The chemical must not be allowed to penetrate behind settings or the brilliancy of the stones will be spoilt. Neither should it be allowed to remain on the hands or they will be badly stained.

Alloyed gold can be darkened in the same way, only it is necessary to warm the metal until it is almost too hot to handle or the sulphide will not act upon it. Gold of 9, 12, 15 carat can be darkened by heat alone, and often takes the most beautiful shade of purple if the heating is arrested at the right moment.

Copper can be darkened either by the ammonium sulphide or by heat, and if brushed over while warm with a stiff brush and a very little pure beeswax will keep its lustre and colour unchanged for a long time. In gold work of any intricacy it is often difficult and sometimes impossible to polish the inner portions of the ornament, and when finished the work looks unpleasant and incomplete. This difficulty can be obviated by first slightly gilding the whole work, and then polishing it in the ordinary way. A recipe for this is given at the end of the book.

CHAPTER XXIX

Methods of Gilding—Mercury Gilding

MERCURY gilding is done by means of an amalgam of gold with mercury. It is the oldest way of gilding, and is still the best, because the gold is carried into the surface of the metal, and is not merely a thin skin more or less adherent.

Take 8 parts of mercury and one part of fine gold. Put the gold into a small crucible and heat it on the forge with a blow-pipe, and when the crucible reddens pour in the mercury, and stir it into the gold with an iron rod until you have a pasty mass. Empty the crucible into a bowl of clean water, and wash the amalgam carefully by kneading it with the thumb and finger against the sides of the vessel. This is to get rid of the excess of mercury. Then take the amalgam, place it in a bit of chamois leather, and squeeze out the remainder of the uncombined mercury. Because this excess of mercury contains a portion of gold it should be kept separate, and used when you wish to make amalgam again.

Next dissolve mercury in pure nitric acid in the proportion of 10 parts of mercury to 11 of nitric acid; dilute the solution with twenty times its mass of water, shake the mixture well, and keep it in a stoppered bottle for use.

Boil out the objects you wish to gild, and remove all grease with hot soda, and dip the work in the solution of nitrate of mercury. Take a small scratch-brush of brass wire, dip it first in the solution, and then take up a small portion of the amalgam, and spread it carefully and evenly over the whole surface to be gilded.

Some workers mix the amalgam and the nitrate of mercury together, and dip the object to be gilded in the mixture. The first method is probably less waste-

238

ful. Then hold the work over a charcoal brazier placed in a fireplace with a glass screen across the opening. This enables you to see the progress of the evaporation without the danger of inhaling the vapour of mercury. The work should not be laid on the coals, but in an iron pan or on an iron plate over the coals. When the mercury has evaporated rub the object with a soft brush, and polish with the scratch-brush and a little stale beer, or with rouge and water on the buff. If the work appears spotty, drop a little strong nitric acid on the spots, afterwards plunge the whole object in weak pickle (5 of water to one of acid), and then touch the defective portions with fresh amalgam, and evaporate as before.

Another method is to soak linen rags in a solution of chloride of gold. Dry and burn the rags, carefully preserving the ashes. Thoroughly clean the object you wish to gild, and rub the ashes with a bit of damp leather over the surface. Continue this until you see the gold-colour appear; then wash the object well, and burnish the surface with a highly polished burnisher. The washings and every particle of the ashes should be carefully kept because they contain minute quantities of gold which can all be recovered when desired Other methods are given in the appendix.

CHAPTER XXX

A Method of Shaping and Cutting the Softer Precious Stones — The Stones most easily Cut — The Cements Required—Drilling Stone—The Engraver's Lathe—Polishing.

THE softer precious stones, such as moonstones, opals, chrysoprase, peridot, and turquoise, may be shaped either with the corundum file and water, or with emery-wheels fixed on a polishing-spindle. In the latter case it will be necessary to have a water-can, with a tiny tap soldered in the bottom, hung over the emery-wheel in such a way that a drop of water may fall on the wheel at frequent intervals while you are grinding. To protect yourself from being splashed, you will need a metal catch-pan, which will collect the drip and the water which flies from the wheel. The stone to be shaped must be fixed on the end of a rod of wood about as thick as a pencil and 8 inches long. Many people use cane for this purpose; being flexible, it is less likely to jar the

240

stone when the latter is pressed against the wheel; but a piece of common firewood will do just as well. Warm a lump of ordinary graver's cement, and mould it on the end of the stick with a wetted finger to a roughly conical shape (fig. 155). Warm the end again, and press the stone, also slightly warmed, into the end of the cement, and mould the cement closely round it with the finger. When cool, the stone can be pressed against the wheel and shaped to whatever form you please. A fine surface can be given on a wheel of finer grain and the stone polished on a leather buff with fine emery and water, finishing up on another buff with putty powder and water. If the stone is very tender, as, for example, opals often are, it may be well to use what is called soft cement for fixing the stone to the polishing-stick. This is made of finely sifted wood ashes, well

FIG. 155.

Q   241

kneaded into melted suet until the required consistency is obtained.

Stones can be slit by using a bow made
out of a tapered rod of ash about 2 feet
long strung with iron wire. The wire
is fastened 4 inches away from the butt,
so that the latter may be used as a handle.
This wire, anointed with emery, is used
as a saw. Much patience is needed, as it
cuts very slowly. A quicker result is obtained by cutting out a disc of soft iron
and using it as a circular saw, with oil and
emery. A lapidary's slitter is merely a larger
disc used horizontally. The defect of the
small iron disc is that it is difficult to get
a clean cut with it. Still, for cutting
turquoise or opal matrix it does well
enough, if worked steadily and with
patience. The stone to be slit should
be cemented to a block of wood instead
of a stick, and the block firmly secured
to the table of the polishing-lathe, yet
in such a way that it may be pressed
gradually against the edge of the wheel
as the latter slowly cuts its way through
the stone. It is useless to attempt to
hasten the process. The least hurry may
easily ruin a good stone. The advantage
of the methods just described is that they

are within the reach of any one, and with care can be made to produce very good results. It must be remembered that native workers in the East do their work with tools even more rudimentary than these.

For drilling stones, a drilling or seal-engraver's lathehead will be needed, as it is important that the drill should revolve with great speed and steadiness. This lathehead is a simple pillar of iron or brass, with a small wheel revolving in a slot. The axle of the wheel is a steel tube working in tin bearings. The drills and cutting tools are fixed in this tube with melted tin or lead. The drills themselves are small tubes of iron, and the cut is given by means of diamond dust. Small rods, with variously shaped ends, taper knobs of different sizes, and tiny wheels, are used, with diamond dust to give a cutting surface, in engraving seals.

By using small wheels of thick copper screwed on the spindle of the polishing-lathe, some of the harder stones can be shaped with oil and emery, and polished on similar wheels of tin, the final polishing being done on wheels of wood or with fine emery, followed by leather and

243

putty powder; but, if any considerable
amount of work is required, it is better to
get hold of an intelligent lapidary, who
will cut the stones for you much more
quickly than you could.

CHAPTER XXXI

Piece-Moulding—The Model—The Casting-Flasks
—The Sand—Filling the Flasks—Making the
Mould—The Charcoal—The False Cores—The
Back Mould—The Core of the Model—Arrang-
ing the Gates—Drying the Mould.

Piece-
Moulding

WORK that is undercut, or in any way
complicated, can only be cast by piece-
moulding or by the waste-wax process.
Suppose it necessary, for example, to make
a piece-mould cast of the symbol of St.
Luke designed as one of the feet of a cross
or candlestick. First make your model
in wax or clay, and take a cast of it in
plaster of Paris. Next take a pair of casting-flasks, large enough to hold the model
and give plenty of room for the pour of
the metal. Lay the lower or eye portion
of the flask on a flat board, and fill it with
fine casting-sand made very slightly moist.
The sand must be such as will bind well
under pressure. Hampstead sand, which

244

is naturally mixed with a small quantity of fine loam, is very useful for this purpose.

The sand must be well rammed with a mallet into the flask, and great care should be taken to compress the sand well against the sides of the flask, or it may drop out when the mould is turned over. This done, strike off the excess of material with a straight-edge, and adding a few more handfuls of sand, lay a stout board on the top, and drive the sand well in by evenly distributed blows of a mallet. Again strike off the superfluous sand, and lay the model to be cast well within the flask, so that when you make the spout or pour for the metal there may be a good weight of metal above the model. Yet it must not be too far away or you will be in danger of getting a spongy cast, because the metal will have cooled in its passage into the mould. Having fixed the position of the model, take a metal spatula or modelling-tool and excavate a hollow in the sand just large enough to receive half the thickness of the model; lay the model on its back in the hollow, and with some very fine sand fill in underneath the model, so that every part of it is well supported—until, in fact, you have

245

taken a partial impression of the surface.
Now dust some finely powdered brick-dust
from a rough canvas bag—a bag made of
sacking or nailcloth will do perfectly well
for this; with a camel's-hair mop, such as
gilders use, brush this well into the surface,
and blow away all that does not now ad-

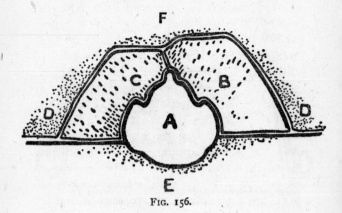

FIG. 156.

here. You will now proceed to make the
false cores. These are movable portions
of the moulds so arranged as to avoid the
undercutting (fig. 156). Again dust the
model A with a little finely powdered French
chalk, and brush the superfluity away with
the camel's-hair mop, and, taking a little
fine sand, press it carefully with the fingers

246

into the interstices of the form, and build the sand up into a block with sloping sides (see fig. 156, B). With a small mallet tap the sand all over evenly, both to drive it home and also to consolidate and

FIG. 157.

shape it. Then with the flat steel spatula or modelling-tool cut away the sand along the line you have chosen for the seam (see fig. 156, F), pare the surface of the block

247

into a regular and even shape. Now stick
a fork made of two thick strong needles
or pointed wires inserted in a slip of hard
wood (see fig. 158) into the block, and
having laid the flask on a flat board, tap
the underside of the board smartly, but
not too vigorously, until you see that
the core has separated slightly from the
model, lift it carefully away, and dust
the moulded surface with finely powdered

FIG. 158.

charcoal from a coarse muslin bag, and
replace the core on the mould ; tap it gently
but firmly home again. Proceed in like
manner with the opposite side of the model
(see fig. 156, C). You will now have to
make the mould for the upper part of
the head. This you will do in the back-
mould, which will be made in the peg
half of the flask (see figs. 156, D and 157).
Place this upper half of the flask in
248

position. Having dusted the whole upper surface of the false cores and the under mould, press some of the finest sand over the top of the head of the model, and then fill the whole mould with ordinary casting-sand and ram it well into place with the mallet handle and afterwards with the head of the mallet. Strike off the superfluity as before, and as before again pile on sand and drive it down with the flat board and the mallet. Now lift the peg half away, and you will have the impression of the false cores (fig. 156, D shows the section of the back-mould) and also a mould of the top of the animal's head, thus completing one-half of the mould. Now dust charcoal over the impression of the head and replace the upper half of the flask. Carefully turn the whole mould over and lift the under half free from the model, leaving the model and the false cores resting in the upper half of the mould. With a spoon or a spatula scoop out two shallow hollows in what are now the upper faces of the false cores. This is to give a register and to enable you to place the false cores in their proper positions when the mould is taken apart (see figs. 157 and 159). Now shake out the sand which

249

FIG. 159.

you had previously beaten into the under
mould, and replacing the frame in position
on the upper flask, dust the mould over
with brick-dust as before, carefully press
fine sand over the back of the model,
then fill in with the ordinary sand, ram
it well home, and fill up the frame as
before. Again lift off the mould, dust
the new impression with charcoal, and
replace the mould. With a knife loosen
all the sand nearly down to the bottom of
the upper flask, and again fill in and ram
the mould completely full. The object
of this is to incorporate the sand and the
charcoal facing. If this be neglected the
cast will be poor, because the charcoal by
itself cannot resist the flow of the metal.
The latter carries away the fine edges and
surfaces, and instead of a smooth cast you
get a rough and ragged one. The mould
is now complete save for the vents and the
pour, if you intend to make a solid casting. If you wish it to be hollow you will
need a core made thus :—

You will take a piece of iron wire, about
$\frac{1}{8}$ inch diameter and 2 inches long, and
place it in the mould against the upper
part of the head of the bull in a little
groove scratched in the surface as shown

251

in the figure. Now take a longer piece of thick wire, just long enough to reach nearly to the bottom of the case and to project 2 inches beyond the head of the bull. Wind it round with a length of thin copper wire to give the sand a better hold, and paint over the whole wire with stiff flour paste. This makes the sand adhere to the wire. Now open the mould, and, having removed the model, replace the false cores in their position, close the mould carefully, and turn it over. Lift off the upper half, and from the opening left between the false cores fill to half its depth with fine sand the place occupied by the model. Now lay the core wire in position, and carefully fill the remaining space with the sand, pressing it into its place against the sides of the mould with a modelling-tool. Take the sand up between your thumb and finger, and use it as if it were modelling-clay, pressing it carefully into place. Now pile on a little more sand to make up that portion of the model which projected above the false cores, and press down the other half of the mould on this, so that the complete model of the bull is built up in sand around the central wire (see fig. 160). This

FIG. 160.

done, cut away the surface of this core
to an even depth of nearly $\frac{1}{8}$ inch. The
depth of the paring fixes the thickness of
the metal in the cast, and that will depend

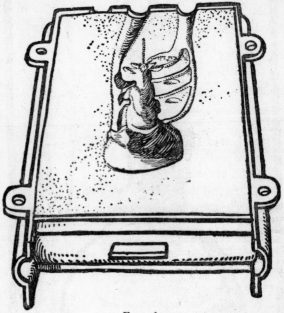

FIG. 161.

on the metal you use. For silver it may,
as above, be a little less than $\frac{1}{8}$ inch;
for bronze or brass it should be rather
more than $\frac{1}{8}$. It will now be necessary

254

to pare the other side of the core, and to do this you must turn the mould over carefully, open it, and remove the false cores with the lifting needles. When you have done this you must now make the gates, the vents, and the pour (see fig. 161). The pour is the principal funnel-shaped opening by which the metal enters the mould, the gates are the smaller openings from the pour to various parts of the mould, and the vents are openings or grooves arranged to let out the air when the metal fills up the mould. It is almost always best to arrange the pour so that the metal enters at the bottom of the mould, and fills it up gradually without risk to the angles and points of sand which project into the mould.

Scrape a deep groove in the surface of each half of the mould, beginning at one of the holes left for that purpose in the end of the flask. You can do this with an old teaspoon

Fig. 162.

255

Piece-
Moulding

or a broad spatula with a rounded end (see fig. 162). The mould is now complete, and needs only to be thoroughly baked near the fire, so that all moisture is driven out.

CHAPTER XXXII

Casting by Waste-Wax Process—The Wax Model—
The Sand—Casting the Mould—Bedding the
Mould in the Flasks—Casting without Flasks—
Hollow Castings—A Third Method of Casting.

Casting by
Waste-Wax
Process

IT is often necessary to cast objects which may be either too small or too complicated for the last process, or that may require a greater delicacy of finish in the cast.

Make your model in casting-wax. This is a composition of fine beeswax, resin, and Venice turpentine in the following proportions: 1 part best pure beeswax, $\frac{1}{12}$th part fine resin, $\frac{1}{8}$th part best Venice turpentine. Melt in an earthen pot, stir well, and add a little colouring matter according to wish or necessity—Venetian red, Prussian blue, or any colour which stains well without having much body in itself.

If the result when cold is too sticky,

remelt it, and add a little more pure wax, as there is an excess of turpentine. If it becomes flaky in working add more turpentine. When worked between the thumb and finger it should draw out into long threads. Another mixture is, two parts of best Japan wax and one part white resin. This gives excellent results, but is rather sticky to work. If the object required be very small you can model it in pure Japanese wax, which can be bought anywhere. Almost any wax, except paraffin wax, will do if on melting it runs away and leaves no solid residue.

Having made your model, roll up a slender rod of the wax, say $\frac{1}{8}$ to $\frac{1}{4}$ inch diameter, and, after warming the end of the rod, attach it to the back, bottom, or any part of the model which will not be seen ultimately. This is to make the funnel or pour. Take the finest casting-sand you can procure, mix it with a very little fine loam, and dry it thoroughly by the fire. Pound it well in a mortar with an iron pestle, and roll it with a smooth wooden roller on a smooth hard board to crush out any uneven lumps. Sift it through a canvas bag, or rub it through a fine sieve. Put a small quantity of this finely powdered

R   257

sand into a cup, and add enough water to
make it into a creamy liquid, and set it on
one side to settle. When the sand has
partly settled to the bottom, pour off the
clearer water, and, taking a soft camel's-
hair brush, paint the sand carefully over
the whole surface of the model. Very little
will stick on at first, but that does not
matter; put the model on one side to dry,
and when dry paint on another coat. Take
care that the coats are laid on evenly, and
avoid bubbles or holes. If these are left
they produce lumps and blots which will
be certain to come in awkward places
on the cast. Fill in the hollows and
crevices first; always leaving each coat to
dry perfectly before laying on another.
When you have covered the whole model
very carefully with, say, seven or eight
coats, the last one being thoroughly dry,
take a flask of suitable size, and partly fill
the eye half with sand, lay the model on
its face, and press the sand well underneath it, so that the sand coating of the
model is everywhere well supported, then
ram the sand well in all around; lay the
peg half in place, and fill that also with
well-rammed sand as before described.
Now lay a board on the back and face of

the mould, clamp all firmly together, and place by the furnace fire to dry. When dry run the wax out, and when it has all run away let the mould get thoroughly hot, so that the remainder of the wax in the mould disappears. Place the mould on the ground, mouth uppermost, so supported that you may pour in the metal previously melted either in a crucible in the furnace or with a gas blow-pipe and foot-bellows on the forge, having first piled coke around the crucible. When cool the mould can now be taken apart, the sand broken away, and the casting finished by chasing.

Small work can be done without flasks. In this case the first process of painting on the sand must be continued until you have got a thickness of at least an inch of sand over every part of the model, except of course the top of the pour or gate for the metal. This mould, after being tied round for greater security with binding-wire, may be dried and used as before described.

The advantages of this method of casting over the ordinary process of waste wax are—1st, that it takes less time; 2nd, the elaborate system of runners and risers to carry off the air in the mould is unneces-

259

sary, the air escapes naturally through the
pores of the sand; 3rd, there are fewer
cracks or fissures in the mould; 4th, the
mould has not to be made red hot before
pouring in the metal. By the method
just described the work is cast solid. If
you wish to have it hollow you must proceed differently. Paint one-half of the
model only with the successive layers of
the sand, and leave the back entirely uncovered. When the sand is fully dry dust
a little French chalk over the wax, and
take a pair of flasks, and fill the eye half
as described for piece-moulds. Lay the
model so that there will be a sufficient
length of pour above it, and excavate the
sand so that the uncovered half of the
model may rest in it. Pack fine sand well
underneath this, and place the peg half
of the flask in position. Having dusted
brick-dust all over the face of the mould,
ram fine sand all round the model, fill the
mould, and strike off clean as before.

Reverse the mould, and lift off the eye
half, shake out the sand, dust the model
clean, and, taking pinches of fine sand,
press them into the cracks and crannies of
the latter. Then ram the sand well over
the mould and into the sides of the flask,

and level the surface as before. Open the mould again, dust the impression with charcoal, close the mould, and again loosen the sand over the model. Ram in more sand until the frame is full. Now place the mould mouth downwards near the furnace, set a small vessel underneath to catch the wax. When the mould is hot and all the wax has run away, open the mould, take a length of iron wire, just long enough to traverse the whole model lengthwise and project an inch at each end, and, having coiled fine copper or iron wire round it, rub a little flour paste over it, and make a core of sand round the wire; lay it in position so that as far as possible there may be an equal space all round it. When the core is dry you can fix it in position and pour in the metal.

There is yet another way of casting hollow figures by the waste-wax process.

A matrix of the figure is made in gelatine (this part of the work is best done by a plaster moulder), melted wax is painted in, and the mould is turned about every way, so that every part of the mould receives an even coating of wax. This coating should be a little more than ⅛ inch thick. When the wax is quite cold it is taken out of the mould. You will now have a hollow casting in wax, we will suppose, of the bull. Fix the rod of wax for the pour at the back of the model. Run a stout iron wire lengthwise through the model (see fig. 159). This is to carry the core. Coat the wax with the sand and water as before, and, when thick enough, bed the resulting mould in the flasks, ram the sand round the core wire, melt the wax out, and cast the figure. When cast the core can be removed bit by bit from the bottom. The iron rod, which will be firmly fixed in the cast, must also be removed, the hole left by it filled up with metal, and the head then chased to remove traces of the join.

CHAPTER XXXIII

On Old Work and Old Methods.

WHAT most impresses the student of all old work of the best periods is the clear shining sincerity of the worker and his patient skill. The worker's hand travelled

262

lovingly over every part of the work, giving
it a kindliness of aspect enduringly attractive.   More than this it bears a touching
witness to the spirit of the worker.[1]   What
that spirit was, the preface by the eleventh-
century monk, Theophilus, to his work on
" Divers Arts," more clearly shows us :—

"Most dear brother, moved by sincere
love I have not delayed to insinuate to thy
mind how much honour and perfection
there is in avoiding idleness, and in tramp-
ling down slackness and sloth ; and how
sweet and pleasant it is to be occupied in
works of divers utility.   In the words of a
certain orator, 'To know aught is a merit,
it is a fault not to desire to learn.'   Nor let
any one delay to learn of them of whom
Solomon saith, 'Whoso increaseth knowledge increaseth work,' because the diligent
in meditation can understand what growth
of mind and body proceedeth thence.

"For it is clearer than light that whoso
seeketh ease and levity giveth occasion to
unprofitable stories, scurrile talk, curiosity,

---

[1] Cellini is not a case in point.   Moreover his art has
been greatly over-rated.   It is in most cases meretricious
in the true sense of the word.   At the same time, he
was an amazing blackguard, which perhaps accounts
for his immortality.

263

wine-bibbing, drunkenness, brawls, fights, homicide, bawdiness, theft, sacrilege and perjury, and the like, which things are pernicious in the eyes of God, who regardeth the humble and quiet man working in silence, in the fear of the Lord, obedient to the precept of the blessed Apostle Paul, 'But rather let him labour with his hands the thing that is good, that he may have to give to him that needeth.'

"I, desiring to be an imitator of this man, drew near to the porch of Holy Wisdom, and beheld a little chapel full of divers colours of every variety displaying the use and nature of each. Having with unseen footsteps quickly entered therein, I filled up the aumbry of my heart with a sufficiency of all things, and having tried them one by one by diligent experiment, and having proved all by the eye and hand, I commend them without envy to thy study."

Again, in another place, Theophilus thus admonishes the worker :—"Whatsoever thou art able to learn, understand, or devise in the Arts is ministered to thee by the grace of the sevenfold spirit.

"By the Spirit of Wisdom thou knowest that all created things come of God, and

264

without Him there is nothing. By the
Spirit of Understanding thou acquirest
capacity of mind in what order, variety,
and proportion thou mayest avail to apply
thyself to the different work. By the
Spirit of Counsel thou dost not conceal
the talent conceded thee by God, but with
humility, working and teaching openly,
thou revealest faithfully to those earnestly
desirous of knowledge. By the Spirit of
Fortitude thou dost shake off the torpor
of sloth, not beginning aught with slackness thou dost carry it through with all
thy power to the end. By the Spirit of
Knowledge conceded to thee thou dost
dominate with thy genius by reason of the
fullness of thy heart, and that of which
thy mind is full thou dost utter boldly in
public. By the Spirit of Piety thou dost
govern what, for whom, why, how much,
and in what manner thou workest, and
through pious consideration, lest the vice
of avarice or covetousness creep in, thou
shalt moderate the price of thy reward.
By the Spirit of the Fear of the Lord thou
art mindful that thou canst do nothing of
thyself, nor dost thou think to have, or
to desire, aught but by the gift of God,
but believing, confessing, and giving thanks

265

whatsoever thou knowest, whatsoever thou
art or may be, thou dost ascribe to the
Divine Mercy."

This most delightful person, moreover,
was a thorough craftsman, and knew intimately what he wrote about. And he
described his work as only a good workman could, who was at the same time
skilled with his pen.

Here, for example, is his description of
making casts of handles for a chalice by
the waste-wax process.

"Take wax and form handles thereof,
and model on them dragons, or beasts, or
birds, or leaves in whatsoever way thou
wishest. On the top of each handle, however, place a little wax, rolled round like
a slender candle, as long as the little
finger, the upper end being somewhat
larger. This is called the 'pour'; this thou
wilt fix to the handle with a warm tool.

"Then take well-beaten clay and cover
up each handle separately, so that all the
hollows of the modelling may be filled
up. When they are dry, again coat evenly
over all, and in like manner a third time.
Afterwards put these moulds near the
coals, so that when they get hot thou
mayest pour out the wax. The wax being

266

poured out, place them wholly in the fire, turning the mouth of the moulds by which the wax ran out downwards. When they glow like coals, then melt the silver, adding to it a little Spanish brass. If, for example, there be 4 ounces of silver, add a quarter of an ounce of brass, but if more or less, then in proportion to the weight. Taking the moulds out of the fire, stand them firmly up, and pour in the silver at those places where thou pouredst out the wax. When they shall have cooled, break away the clay, and with files and scorpers join them to the chalice."

There is no reason why this process should not be applied by any student to-day. The one thing needful to ensure success is to get a loamy clay, which will not shrink or crack too much when the mould is fired. Otherwise the process is identical with modern practice.

Again, in his description of moulds for stamped work :—

"Iron stamps may be made of the thickness of one finger, the width of three or four fingers, and one finger long. They must be sound, and without flaw or fissure on the upper face. In this face thou wilt engrave with the scorpers in the same way

267

as for seals, broad and narrow borders of
flowers (see fig. 164), beasts, and little birds,
or dragons, with necks and tails coiled
together. They must not be engraved
too deeply, but moderately, and with care.
Then thou thinnest out silver as long as thou
needest, and much thinner than for repoussé

work, and thou dost
clean it with powdered
charcoal, and with a
cloth dost polish it with
chalk scraped over the
metal. This done fix
thou the silver plate
over any border, and
having laid the iron
upon the anvil with the
sculptured side upper-
most, and having laid

FIG. 163.

the silver over the sculpture, place a thick
piece of lead over the silver, strike strongly
with the hammer, so that the lead may
impinge on the thin silver and drive it so
forcibly into the sculpture that every trace
of it may be clearly seen.

"If the plate be longer than the mould
draw it from place to place, and hold it
evenly on the iron with the pincers, so
that when one part has been struck up

268

another may be struck, and so on, until
the plate has been filled up. This work
is useful enough when thou art making
borders for altar tables, for pulpits, for
shrines for the bodies of the saints, for the
covers of books, and in whatever places
the work may be needed. When the
relief is suitable and slight it is easily
done. Thou canst do likewise with copper
similarly thinned, gilded, and polished.
Being laid on the iron, gilt side downwards, the lead is laid over it, and hammered until the pattern is visible. The
image of the crucified Lord is also engraved in iron, as described above, and
being stamped on silver or gilt copper,
they make therewith phylacteries or re-
liquaries and little shrines of the saints.
The image of the Lamb of God is also
carved in iron, and the figures of the four
Evangelists. The impresses of these on
gold or silver are used to decorate bowls
of precious wood, the image of the Lamb
standing in the midst of the vials, the
four Evangelists ranged about in the shape
of a cross. Images of little fishes, birds,
and beasts are also made, which, being
fixed on the rest of the ground of the
bowl, give a very rich effect. An image

269

of the Majesty is made in like manner, and other images of any form or sex. These being stamped in gold or silver or gilt copper give the greatest seemliness to those places on which they are fixed by reason of their delicacy and elaboration. Images of kings and knights are made in the same way, with which, being stamped out of Spanish brass, basins whence water is poured on the hands are ornamented, in the same manner as cups are ornamented with the stamped work in gold and silver. They may have borders in the same metal in which are little beasts or birds or little flowers, which are not fixed together but soldered with tin."

Nothing could be clearer or more practical than this. The result of the process can be seen in the shrine of the bell shown on Plate V. The delightful flower borders on the face of the shrine are all produced in the way described.

Again, the description by Theophilus of the cutting punches, their use, and the employment of the results produced, is a model of clearness :—

" Iron punches are made as long as the finger, thick at one end, and tapering to the other (see fig. 165). They may be filed

270

square, three-cornered, or round, and made
of convenient bigness. The smaller ends
are afterwards case-hardened. Then little
flowers are engraved out of the smaller ends
in such a way that a cutting edge is left
round the border of the flower (fig. 166).
Thin silver or gilded copper
is polished on the upper face
as described above, is thinly
tinned on the lower with
the soldering bit used for
soldering windows, then,
laying thick lead on the
anvil, place thereon the silver
or gilt copper, so that the
gilding may be uppermost
and the tinning underneath;
having taken which punch
thou pleasest, lay the carved
end on the silver, and strike
with the hammer so that
the design may appear and
be at the same time cut
out by the sharp edge of the punch (see
fig. 166).

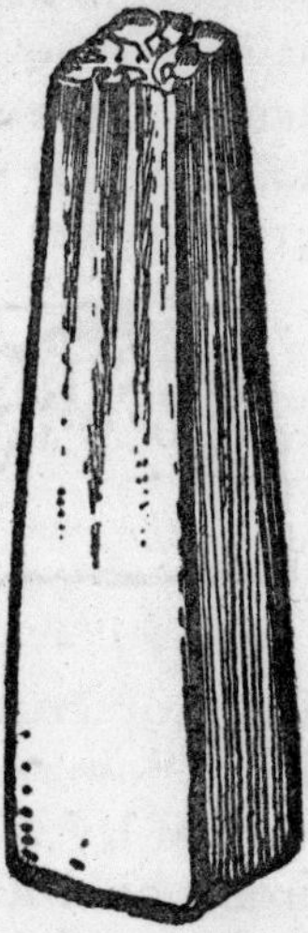

FIG. 164.

"When thou hast stamped out all the
silver keep the flowers by thee; they will
be the heads of nails, the shanks of which
thou wilt make thus: Mix two parts of tin

271

and one of lead together, beat it out thin
and long, and draw it through the draw-
plate, so that thou hast a very long wire
not too slender. Afterwards make for
thyself a slender iron, about 6 inches long,
which is broadened out at one end and
hollowed a little to receive the head of the
nail. The other end is fixed in a wooden
handle. Then sitting near the furnace suitable for this work, before which stands a
little copper vessel full of melted wax,[1]

FIG. 165.

holding the slender iron
in the left hand, the
broader part being heated,
and in the right the tin
wire rolled up like a ball,
dip the end of the wire
in the wax, and, plac-
ing it upon the tinned side of one of the
little flowers so that it may stick, lift it
up and lay it in the hollow of the heated
iron ; hold it there until the metal runs,
and immediately remove it from the fire,
and when cold snip off a length of wire
according to the length thou desirest for
the nail."

The beaded wire so beautiful in its
slight irregularities, seen in Anglo-Saxon

[1] Resin would do just as well as wax.

272

brooches as well as in many of the Greek ornaments, was produced by the beading-tool which Theophilus describes as follows :—

"There is an iron instrument called the beading-tool, which consists of two irons, one above and one below. The lower part is as broad and as thick as the middle

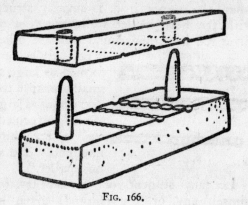

FIG. 166.

finger, and is somewhat thin. In it are two spikes by which it is fixed to wood below, and out of the upper face rise two thick pegs which fit into the upper part of the iron. And this upper iron is of the same size and length as the lower, and is pierced with two holes, one at each end, which receives the two pegs of the lower,

s 273

so that they can be joined together. They must be joined very closely with the file, and in both faces thou wilt groove out several rows of little pits in such a way that when the irons are joined together a hole may appear (see figs. 167, 168). In the large grooves place thou gold or silver rods beaten out long and smoothly round, and when the upper iron is smartly struck with the horn mallet while the gold or silver rod is turned round with the other hand, grains are formed as large as small beans; in the next grains as large as peas are formed; and in the third like lentils, and so on smaller."

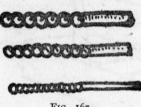

FIG. 167.

Let any student or worker try for himself any of the methods given by Theophilus, and he will find that he is brought into touch with sources of suggestion and ideas of the utmost value to him in his work. It is like stepping from the close atmosphere of a cramped workroom to the freer air of a new world. In fact, the more one compares the work of the past with the work of the present

274

day, the more one is convinced that the design in the past was the outcome of work. To-day the cart is placed before the horse ; work is the outcome of design, hence its thin and meagre aspect. This meagreness may not be remedied, as many think, by wild struggles after originality. They lead but to the eccentric and the morbid. Let the worker be faithful to himself, sincere in his craft, incessant in study, and, unconsciously but surely, his work will express that personal note which sooner or later will win him a place in the choir of artists.

Again, if we look at the work of the Japanese, with their patinæ, their inlays, and incrustations, their many kinds of groundwork, their alloys, inexpensive, but most beautiful, the rich effects they will produce with an incredibly small quantity of gold or silver, and, perhaps more astonishing than all, their beautiful cast work, one realises that there is a whole world of new methods and new materials for study, any one of these worth a lifetime of study, yet not one of them is practised by us. The Japanese as a race are more sensitive than any other to the suggestive beauty of things called common

by the heedless Western. A water-worn
pebble, a strangely marked stone, are
wrought and polished and added to until
it is difficult to say whether the work is
entirely the result of human intention or is
the product of some kind of natural magic,
or is the work of some more than human
artificer. In their metal work, each metal,
native or alloyed, is allied with some other,
at once its foil and quiet emphasis. The
very names of their surfacings reveal an
intensity of observation unknown to us :
" pear-skin ground, millet seed, stone-
dimpled, wood-grain ground, fish-roe
ground, the toad's-back ground," and
many others. They show a knowledge and
a love of surface quality not even dreamed
of by the Western workman wallowing in
the trough of commercialism. Their alloys
are made, not merely with an eye to beautiful colour in the metal itself, but for the
colour and quality of the film of oxide
produced by time or chemicals. Everything they do reveals that intimate inherited knowledge which comes of centuries
of study of the nature and properties of
the materials used. Their workmanship
itself is no less perfect.

In Japan, as indeed everywhere, the

supreme test of good workmanship was that every tool-stroke should be complete in itself and need no retouching. This holds good even when applied to art so widely different as Anglo-Saxon gold work. Whether we look at brooches, buckles, or necklaces, there is the same unhesitating skill, the same quiet perfection of work. Yet the design of any jewel resolves itself, in almost every instance, into the repetition of forms made up of variously twisted, ribbed, or beaded wires laid side by side, or little coils or shapes of wire soldered on the surface, and filled up with tiny grains almost in the Etruscan or Greek manner. The side view of the Alfred jewel (fig. 169) is one illustration of this, while the Anglo-Saxon

FIG. 168.

277

brooches and buckles in the collotype plates
show other very beautiful examples of the
rich results produced by simple means.
Comparative study of the goldsmith's art
shows, amongst other things, the extraordinary persistence of primitive methods
of workmanship and design even down
to the present day. The method of
producing grains, discovered probably by
the first gold worker, and described in
a former chapter, is still used by every
goldsmith in the world; so also the
various patterns of twisted wire. The
use of punches, moulds, and dies are all
primitive methods of enduring utility.
They are, as it were, the terms in the
artist's vocabulary, and it would be just
as impossible to invent a new language
as to discover new methods of work or a
new art.

All through Etruscan, Roman, Italian
art one can trace the methods per-
fected, if not invented, by Greek
artificers, while the influence of Greek
art can be seen even to-day in the work
of the Persian and Indian goldsmith as
well as in those of early Ireland and
Anglo-Saxon England. Again, in early
French art, some beautiful examples of

278

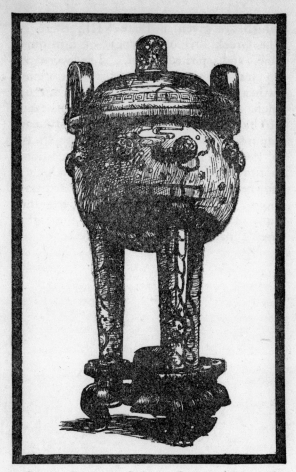

CHINESE BOWL AND COVER IN CLOISONNÉ ENAMEL.

This sample from the Victoria and Albert Museum shows how admirably the Chinese artist has overcome the difficulty of mounting the enamel bowl and cover by providing in each case a broad rim of plain metal. The junction between the fold of enamel and the broad band is managed by raising the cloisons near the rim, so that the metal structure is felt to be carried into the enamel ground.

which are given in Plate VIII., there is
the Greek love of clearness, of firm outline, and spirited form. The work is
so clean, so airy and bright, that it seems
rather the handiwork of angels than of
men. It is a spiritual refreshment even
to look at such things, and the student
cannot spend too much time in the study
of them. He will always find suggestion,
not of new forms, but of untried methods;
not new design, but hints of new expres-
sions; he will learn what is indeed the
sum of the whole matter, that the right
use of material leads to right ideas.

THIRTEENTH-CENTURY FRENCH PRICKET CANDLESTICK,
FROM THE BRITISH MUSEUM.

The romantic beauty of this small master-work and the romantic
use of crystal and gilt bronze will be sufficiently obvious to
those who have studied the original to make further description unnecessary.

THE new section which follows contains chapters on Japanese metal work and processes of metal colouring, which are based on demonstrations privately given by Professor Unno Bisei to the author and his pupils.

CHAPTER XXXIV

To beat up a Vase out of a Sheet of Metal.

FIRST measure the distance from A to D (fig. 169), and take that as the radius of the circle of metal which will be required. The thickness should be about 12 gauge.

283

The metal disc is next annealed and cleaned by being dipped in the sulphuric pickle. Mark with compasses the bottom

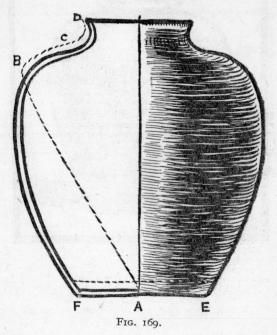

FIG. 169.

circle EF. Then take the metal and a wedge-shaped boxwood mallet, and having a stake the shape of fig. 170, set the metal against the tip of the stake, so that the edge of the stake just comes to the edge of the circle (fig. 170), and begin to beat the metal away from you round the circle,

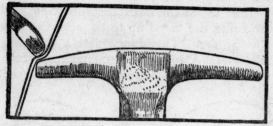

Fig. 170.

being very careful to keep to the line. Having completed the circle, repeat the process a little higher up, and follow round always in circles, until the top or outer edge is reached. The metal should now be re-annealed, and the process

Fig. 171.

repeated from the beginning until the work looks in section like fig. 171. At this stage continue the work on a stake

285

To beat up a
Vase out of
a Sheet of
Metal like fig. **13,** taking care always not to let
the tip of the stake jar on the bottom
of the vase, as that will stretch and split
the metal at this point.

The use of the last stake will enable you
to bring the metal up to the shape shown
in fig. 172. This done, mark a circle on
the metal A and B, fig. 169, taking a stake
shaped as fig. 173A. and begin to draw the

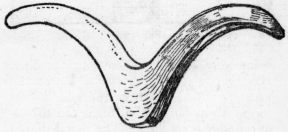

FIG. 13 (*on p.* 54).

metal in to form the neck. At this stage
the work must be annealed more frequently
and great care exercised, as the metal is
more likely to split. By beating from
BC the rest of the curve CD will take
its own shape with very little beating.

Before beginning to beat on the stake
(fig. 173), it will be advisable to make
a template of the section. A hammer
286

like fig. 174 should be substituted for the mallet, as the metal requires heavier beating in order to compress it into

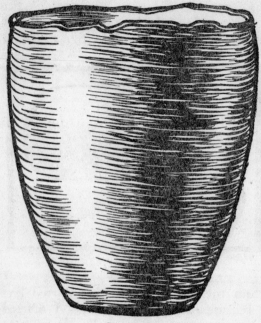

FIG. 172.

shape, and then to stretch it again to form the neck.

When the required shape has been

287

To beat up a
Vase out of
a Sheet of
Metal
obtained, the work must be planished smooth all over, beginning at the base with a flat, round stake like fig. 175, using a flat, round-faced hammer like fig. 175A.

The angle of the base is to be planished true on a stake shown in fig. 170, and

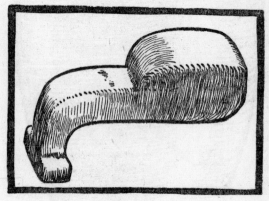

FIG. 173.

from the angle " F " to the dotted line " B " use a stake like figs. 173 or 176, fixed into a long straight arm. The neck is next planished with a cushion-faced hammer (fig. 177) on hollow stakes (figs. 178–9), fixed as the previous one was in the long arm. The use of the cushion-faced

288

hammer is to enable you to get into the
quick curve of the neck of the vase.

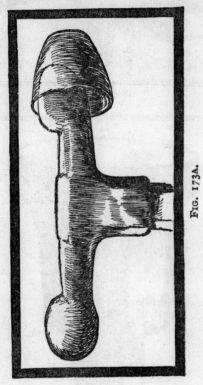

To get a smooth, even surface the

To beat up a
Vase out of
a Sheet of
Metal

FIG. 174.

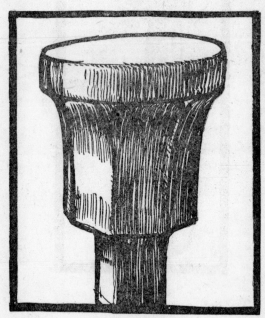

FIG. 175.

metal must be planished three or four times, annealing after each planishing.

When hammering, keep the blows in circles round the vase. This can be done by marking a few faint lines on the surface with the compasses. The lines must be very faint, as if they are at all

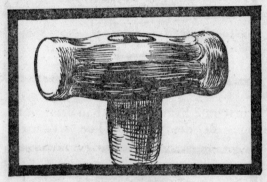

FIG. 175A.

deep, it will be difficult to planish them out.

When the vase is smooth and shapely, polish it with fine sand-paper, then brush it on the lathe with pumice and oil, and proceed to crocus and rouge if the vase is of silver. If it is of copper, finish off with whiting.

291

To beat up a
Vase out of
a Sheet of
Metal In this, as in all craft work, more
will be learnt from a few lessons from

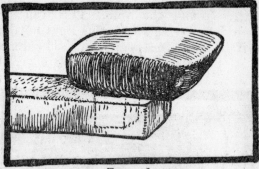

FIG. 176.

a first-rate hammerman than from many
pages of description. The student is

FIG. 177.

advised, therefore, to take the earliest
opportunity of getting a practical de-

292

monstration of the process from a skilled workman.

FIG. 178.

FIG. 179.

CHAPTER XXXV

To make a Card Case.

A CARD Case may be made thus :—

Procure an iron die of the size and shape required.

File up the top surface to the shape of one half of the box (see A, fig. 180).

This is the punch from which the blanks are to be stamped. Make a mould by pouring molten tin into an iron shape not less than 1 inch larger all round than the top of the iron die and not less than 1 inch deep; lay this on a flat sheet of iron and lute the joints all round with whiting. Lead and pewter are often used, but tin is better because it is harder. While the tin is cooling but still molten, press the iron die therein, so that it may make an impression $\frac{1}{4}$ inch deep. When cool, the die can be hammered in to make the impression clean and smooth (see B, fig. 180).

The shell should now be cut out of sheet silver, squared up, the corners cut

294

off, annealed, then tapped into shape over
the iron block with a mallet. When re-
annealed, it may be driven into the tin

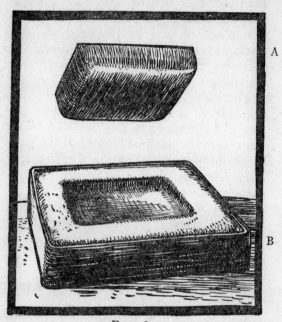

A

B

FIG. 180.

block with the iron die, using a heavy
hammer.

Both sides of the case are treated in
this way and, being stamped up from the

295

same die, can be made to fit together
without difficulty.

After stamping, the shells should be
annealed and cut to size. To prevent
warping during the process of annealing,
iron plates should be prepared $\frac{1}{16}$ inch
thick, cut to size and tapped into shape
over the iron die, one to fit outside the
shell and one inside.

The inside plate must be gapped along
one side so as to leave spaces where the
joints of the hinge will come. The shell
must now be clamped securely at each
corner between these two iron plates with
screw clamps, which can be procured at
any ironmonger's.

This done, the shells can be annealed,
then restamped, reannealed,
and the edges filed true so
that the two halves will fit
together.

The facings to each half may
now be fixed.

FIG. 181.

These are stiffening pieces of
one-eighth square silver wire
soldered to the inner edge of the shell all
round (see A, fig. 181).

When soldered the edges must be filed
true and ground perfectly flat on the stone

296

until the two halves fit together so that the joint is hardly perceptible.

The chenier for the hinge should now be made.

Take a strip of silver, gauge 4, a little more than three times the outside diameter of the tube you require (in this case three thirty-seconds of an inch); file the two edges parallel and cut off two long corners to form a point. Then with the thin pane of a riveting hammer tap the strip into a small groove in the swage block; it will then form a long half-tube. Reanneal, gently close the two edges with a hammer, thus forming a complete tube, and anneal again. It is now ready to draw down to the size required, care being taken that the chenier is drawn perfectly straight and that the line of the joint is not allowed to become spiral. The thin line of the join should then be carefully nicked with a fine three-square file along its length, that being the side to solder down on the case. You must now cut this up into an equal number of parts, 4, 6, or 8, and carefully file the ends in a joint tool, leaving the pieces you intend for the ends of the hinge rather longer than the rest.

This done, graver's cement should be melted into each of the two halves and the two cemented together so that the back edge may be filed out with the joint file. This may be done very carefully by hand, or begun by hand and finished off by fixing a long joint file of the proper size in the chuck of a lathe and then running the case to and fro along it lengthwise as the lathe revolves, so that the groove is deepened evenly and truly along its whole length.

When it is deep enough to receive the joint, which should not be let in too deeply or the case may not open as widely as you would wish, take the case apart, and clean off the cement.

Take the case, and holding it firmly in the left hand, place the joints in position along the groove, and with a fine pencil-point mark on the shells the position of each joint, then remove the top half of case, leaving all the cheniers resting in the groove. Take a piece of fine binding-wire and tie the first joint in position; do the same with each alternate one. If the number of joints is six there will be three on each half, the two end cheniers being on opposite sides.

298

Having boraxed the joints to be soldered, knock out very carefully those you have not tied, place your thin paillons of solder and apply a gentle heat so that the borax may dry without disturbing the various sections of the joint. This done, using a soft flame all over the body of the case, continue blowing until the solder flushes along the length of the joint.

It should then be pickled before arranging the joints on the other side. When you have the second lot of cheniers in place, before soldering gently try them to see if they fit opposite to those in the soldered half. If they are quite right, solder as before. It is important to bear in mind that the join of the chenier must be soldered downwards in the groove.

The whole work may now be whitened, stoned, and polished, but before doing this any fittings required for springs, catches, attachments for elastic bands, card holders, &c., must be prepared and fixed.

The spring for the joint should now be made.

Procure from any of the shops for silver-smiths a few lengths of fine watch-spring of such a size that three will go inside

the joint (see fig. 182). If the joint is
very small one spring will do, but three
are better. Put the case together, pass the springs down
through the joint, and plug
firmly at the end with small
silver wedges.

Plug

FIG. 182.

Then holding the case firmly in one
hand, having the hinge edge away from
you, grip the springs with the pliers and
turn them towards you for at least half
a turn, then get the boy or assistant to
plug the free end with another wedge of
silver and file off the ends clean. The
springs can be fixed single-handed if a
piece of smooth, flat wood made securely
to fit inside the case be procured. Having
placed this inside and put a thin board
or thick card on each side of the case,
it can be held in the vice and the springs
can be twisted and plugged without
assistance. The whole can now be
cleaned and polished as you may desire.

The shape may be engraved or inlaid
or damascened, or decorated with niello,
or treated in any way you may please, only
of course all this must be done before
running the pin or springs through the
hinge. If desired the case may be made

300

to open with a catch. In this instance the spring in the joint must be twisted the opposite way, so that the lid may fly open when the catch is released.

The spring catch may be simply a piece of watch-spring as long as the case, with a thumb-piece fixed to the centre. A circular hole should be filed in the lower half just beneath the facing, encroaching somewhat upon its thickness. This hole may be $\frac{1}{8}$ inch in diameter. The thumb-piece would be slightly less in diameter and about $\frac{1}{4}$ inch long. The ends of the spring are retained by small slotted wing-pieces soldered to the inside of the box beneath the edge of the facing.

FIG. 183.

The thumb-piece has a small plate soldered to it. This plate has a projection soldered on the front, and a portion of the plate is turned up at the back just large enough to retain the spring (see figs. 183, 184, 185). The thumb-piece is pushed through the hole from the inside and the spring slipped into the slot at the back. The projection on the front of the thumb-plate is so adjusted that it may

301

To make a
Card Case
catch over a prepared projection on the
corresponding facing of the other half.

There are many ways in which spring
catches may be made, and many other
suggestions will present themselves as the
work proceeds. If desired, slotted pieces
of silver may be soldered to each side of
one or other of the halves in which elastic

FIG. 184.   FIG. 185.

bands to hold the cards in place may be
fixed, or a shell of thin silver may be
soldered just within the edge of the facing
as may be desired.

This method of case-making has many
applications, and the process is described
fully because of its applicability in other
directions.

302

CHAPTER XXXVI

Notes on the Whetting and Use of Gravers and
Scorpers.

Notes on the
Whetting
and Use of
Gravers and
Scorpers

(1) A, FIG. 186, shows the blank before
being whetted. This blank is always too
long for ordinary use, so that a portion of
the " tang " or reverse end has to be removed before inserting in the handle. This
is accomplished in the following manner :
Place the blank in a vice with the tang
you wish to break off projecting, then
take a small hammer and strike the tang
sharply. It will be found to break away
quite cleanly.

The tool must now be tempered. Pass
the graver through and through the blue
flame of a small gas jet, until it is a pale
straw colour, then plunge into oil. The
graver is now ready for whetting.

(2) B in fig. 186 gives an illustration of
the most useful whet for general work on
metal, pearl, or ivory.

(3) C in fig. 187 shows the whet for
engraving very fine line work on flat
or convex shapes.

Notes on the
Whetting
and Use of
Gravers and
Scorpers
(4) D in the same figure shows the
whet for engraving on concave surfaces.

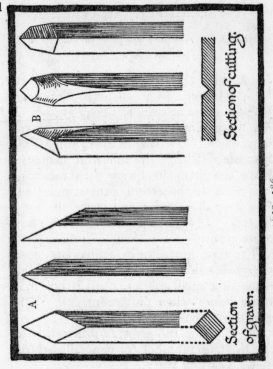

FIG. 186.

This graver should be much shorter
than any other—not more than 4 inches
long including handle, so that the crafts-

304

man may be able to exercise more control over the tool.

(5) E in fig. 188 shows a form of whet

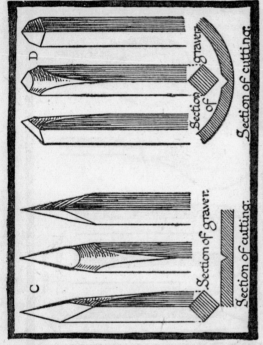

Fig. 187.

used for engraving any long curve on account of the sides of the whet not being of equal inclination. This allows the hand to fall into its natural position

Notes on the
Whetting
and Use of
Gravers and
Scorpers while cutting, viz. slightly to the outside.
Also the top of the whet is slightly in-
clined to the inside. This directs the

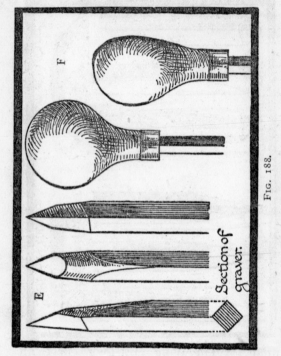

Fig. 188.

spiral chip of metal to the inside of the
curve. This is a very important point.
Unless this is done the chip will turn im-

mediately in front of the graver and thus hide from view the line you are following.

(6) F in fig. 188 illustrates the most

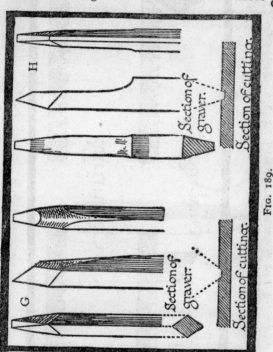

FIG. 189.

useful handle for decorative engraving. It is the ordinary pear-shaped handle, and must be filed to the requisite shape.

Notes on the
Whetting
and Use of
Gravers and
Scorpers

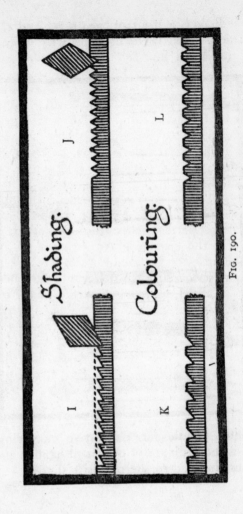

Shading.

Colouring.

J

L

I

K

Fig. 190.

Possessing no sharp edges or angles, this handle can be easily manipulated by the third and fourth fingers, which is often necessary in fine shading.

(7) G in fig. 189 gives the scorper generally used for inscription work, and can be made out of an ordinary graver blank but of lozenge section. In whetting the same rules apply as for the graver, except that a flat surface is added in place of the cutting edge of the graver.

(8) H shows a blank made especially for scorper work which can be bought. It has almost perpendicular sides, but for our purpose the lozenge graver blank is the best, because the inclined sides of the resulting cut give additional richness to the effect.

I and J, fig. 190, illustrate methods of shading a ground by means of parallel lines. Each stroke should be, as it were, cut into or against the stroke which preceded it, the graver being held at a slightly inclined angle (see I, fig. 190). This method produces a contrast of colour in the cutting, whereas the method illustrated at J is more difficult and produces merely a monotonous effect. The same rule applies in colouring (see illustrations K and L).

309

CHAPTER XXXVII

Box-making.

Box-making To make a silver box somewhat similar
methods are required to those outlined
in the last chapter on the card case. A
shape for the lid in iron, a little deeper
than required, should be filed up true.
This may be square, oblong, oval, circular,
or any combination of these shapes, but if
any elaborate pattern is necessary, the iron
die should be as deep as the box and
made so that it can be used as a stake round
which the metal can be tapped to shape.

Assuming, however, that a simple oblong box is required, and that you have
filed up the iron to the desired form
for the lid, take a sheet of silver, gauge
from 10 to 14 according to the subsequent treatment decided upon—10 for
plain work or repoussé, 14 for champlevé, enamel, or niello—mark on it the
shape of the lid, leaving enough metal all
round to form the total height of the sides,
including the lid, and a little to spare to
allow for waste. Cut out the rectangles at

FIG. 197A.—Boss from a Roman Scabbard, showing
decoration in Niello.

See page 315.

the corners so that the metal can be bent
down over the iron shape and meet at the
angles to form the box (see figs. 191, 195).
If it be desired that the box should have a
rounded or slightly domed top, the angles
of the inner rectangle must be gapped
with a knife-edged needle-file as shown

FIG. 191.

on the drawing (see fig. 191). The sides
of the rectangles at A and B (see fig. 191)
must now be chamfered, so that when the
box is bent into shape the edges of the
metal will meet in a clean mitre. The
lines forming the rectangle of the top of
the box must now be cut deeply into the
metal on the wrong side with a sharp

311

Box-making router made of a lozenge graver bent at an angle (see fig. 192). This done, lay the metal on the iron stamp and tap the edges down all round until the silver has taken the required shape. Then take a short stake made just the length of the box inside and having a bevelled edge like fig. 193, and if it be square-edged, on this tap the edge of the lid true all round. Use a similar short stake with a rounded edge as

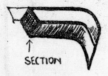

Fig. 192.   Fig. 193.   Fig. 194.

in fig. 194 if the box should have a rounded top. Next tie the box round with binding-wire and solder the angles cleanly and soundly, without using too much solder and taking care to cut the solder up in neat paillons of even size, setting them along the inside of each angle. This done, remove the binding-wire and true up the shape in case it may have got distorted in the flame. Prepare a sheet of silver for the bottom, of the same

312

gauge as that for the sides, and a little
larger all round than the box. The size
of this projection will depend on the
treatment of the box, but a slight projection is always necessary for successful
soldering and clean finish. You will now
mark the position of the joint between the
lid and the body of the box, and with a saw
cut through two angles of the box a little

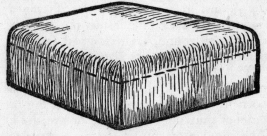

Fig. 195.

way along this line (see fig. 195). This
is to allow the air to escape when soldering.
Scrape the bottom plate all round where
the sides touch it, and tie it and the box
securely together with strong but not
too stout binding-wire. If the wire is
too stout it will bend the box, and damage
may be done in a few seconds that may
take hours to repair. If the wire be

313

too thin it will burn away with the heat required to run the solder. When soldered securely all round, the box and lid may be sawn apart, the meeting edges filed and rubbed down on the flatting-stone until they meet truly all round. The edges of the box must now be thickened. This is done by taking a length of silver wire $\frac{1}{8} \times \frac{1}{16}$ ins. in cross section and fitting a frame of this exactly inside the lid and the box all round, each clamped and soldered securely into its place (see fig. 196).

FIG. 196.

This done, the edge of box and lid must be trued on the face plate, and when both fit together perfectly, the facing or bezel or shutting edge should be prepared. The bezel or facing is simply a strip of thin metal about size 8, fitted to the inside of the facing of the box on three sides, and projecting above it about $\frac{3}{16}$ of an inch, so that the lid fits tightly over it (see fig. 197). The back requires no facing because of the hinge. The bezel must be made just to fit down to the bottom edge of the facing so that it may make a neat finish inside.

FIG. 197.

314

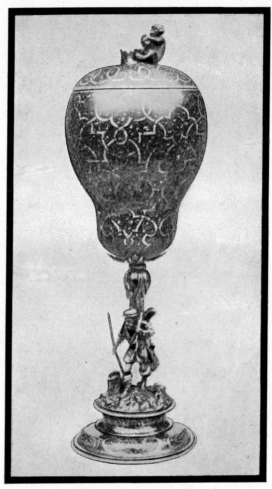

FIG. 198.—Beaten Cup and Cover in Silver and Niello.
From the Museum at Nuremburg.
See page 315.

The joint or hinge can now be prepared.
In this, the procedure described for the
hinge of the card case may be followed,
but hinges similar to those on mediæval
caskets are easy to make and give opportunities of rich decoration. The
subsequent decoration, whether inlay,
champlevé, cloisonné, or engraving, is a
matter for each to decide for himself.

CHAPTER XXXVIII

Niello Work.

NIELLO work is a method of enriching
the surface of gold or other work by first
engraving it and then filling the channels
left by the graver (see figs. 197A and 198)
with a lustrous, black, easily fusible alloy
of silver, lead, copper, and sulphur (see
figs. 197A to 199).

The process is one of very great an-
tiquity. Of its origin and development
nothing is really known save that it is
first found in Egyptian tombs, and has
always been largely used in the East. The
process of manufacture is described by
Pliny and Theophilus and Cellini, and is

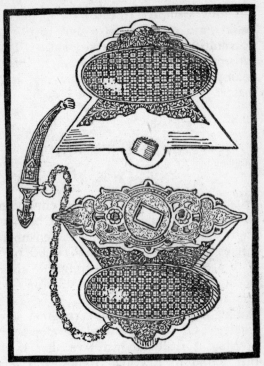

Fig. 199.

found in many books of receipts for gold-
and silver-smith's work.

The following formulæ may be found useful. They are taken by kind permission from the admirable and beautifully illustrated treatise on "Niello" by Herr Marc. Rosenberg, which should be in the hands of every worker :—

Pliny, *Nat. Hist.*, xxxiii. 46.	Silver	. . . 3 parts
	Sulphur	. . 2 „
	Copper	. . . 1 „

Cellini.	Silver	. . . 1 part
	Sulphur	. . half a handful
	Copper	. . . 2 parts
	Lead	. . . 3 „

Augsburg recipe, No. 1.	Silver	. . . 1 part
	Copper	. . . 1 „
	Lead	. . . 2 „

Augsburg recipe, No. 2.	Sulphur	. . 1 part
	Lead	. . . 1 „
	Quicksilver	. 1 „

Rucklin, *Schmuckbuch*, No. 1.	Silver	. . . 3 parts
	Sulphur	. . 6 „
	Copper	. . . 5 „
	Lead	. . . 7 „
	Sal-ammoniac	2 „
	Borax	. . . 24 „

Rucklin, *Schmuckbuch*, No. 2.	Silver	. . . 1 part
	Sulphur	. . 5 parts
	Copper	. . . 2 „
	Lead	. . . 4 „

317

M. E. Vernier in his most inspiring book on "Egyptian Jewellery" gives the following recipes :—

Persian Niello.
Silver	. .	15.30 grms.
Copper	. .	76.00 ,,
Lead	. .	106.00 ,,
Flowers of sulphur	. .	367.00 ,,
Sal-ammoniac		76.00 ,,

Modern French recipe.
Silver	. .	30 parts
Copper	.	72 ,,
Lead	. .	50 ,,
Borax	. .	36 ,,
Sulphur	.	384 ,,

An alloy which I find most useful is prepared as follows :—

Take of fine silver	. . . . . .	6 dwts.	.300
,, ,, copper	. . . . .	2 ,,	.100
,, ,, lead	. . . . .	1 ,,	.050
,, ,, flowers of sulphur	. .	½ oz.	.500

Melt the silver and copper together with a little borax. When well fused, add the lead well covered with sulphur in a screw of tissue paper. Mix the whole thoroughly by stirring with a piece of dry stick. Quickly pour the mixture into a small crucible in which the ½ oz. of sulphur has been placed. The size of the

318

crucible should be what is known as " $\frac{1}{2}$ " size.

Remelt the alloy and pour it out on an iron or steel slab, and while still hot beat it out thin with a hammer. Should it cool before it is thin enough, warm it again with the blow-pipe, and beat it out until it is about 8 in gauge.

I have experimented on all the recipes given above, but only the Persian and modern French recipes gave results which were entirely satisfactory. That given by Cellini is workable but extremely hard.

The work to be decorated should have the parts to be black cleanly cut away with the scorper or graver, as for champlevé work, but the depth of the cutting need not be quite so great.

Should there be, however, any large spaces of black, care must be taken that the ground of these spaces is cut away neatly and evenly. Should this precaution be neglected, portions of the ground will appear through the niello during the finishing processes, and spoil the work. When all is ready, grind up a portion of the prepared niello in an agate mortar, until it is of the fineness of

319

fine sand. Then paint all the portions to be decorated with a weak solution of borax and water,[1] and afterwards with a spatula fill the spaces with the ground niello, mixing it with a very little of the borax solution. This done, remove the surplus water with a piece of blotting paper and gently heat the work in a muffle furnace or with the blow-pipe until the niello melts and runs into the spaces prepared for it. If a blow-pipe be used, the flame must not be allowed to play directly on the niello, as this will cause it to burn and produce cavities and defects in the surface when the work is polished. When the spaces are well filled, and the work is cool, take a sand-paper stick and gently rub the work with it until the silver background everywhere appears. Continue polishing with water of Ayr stone and water, and finish off with the pumice buff. The final polish can be given with crocus and rouge.

Small engraved panels can be done in this way, and when the lines are filled with niello and the whole surface polished they look very beautiful.

[1] Sal-ammoniac may be used instead of borax.

CHAPTER XXXIX

Japanese Methods—Incrustation and Inlay—Of
Inlaying—Simple Inlay : Another Method.

Japanese Methods.

ALL who have seen Japanese gold- and
silver-smiths at work must have been
deeply impressed not only by the simplicity of the tools and methods, but by
the miraculous skill with which these
tools and methods are employed.

I have had the privilege of being in-
structed by Professor Unno Bisei of the
Tokyo Fine Art College, and the following
chapters are based on notes made from
his demonstrations. They have in addition been entirely revised by Professor
Unno himself. The illustrations are from
his own diagrams.

The tools required are (1) a light
chasing-hammer (see fig. 205); (2) a
number of chisels of varying widths
sharpened as shown in figs. 202 to 215.

The whetting of these chisels must be
done with the greatest nicety, as the

x   321

success of this work is largely dependent
on the perfection of the cutting-edge.
In no case should a tool be used when it
is blunt.

Of Inlaying.

A simple piece of inlay such as the
running border **A** (fig. 200) would be done
in this way.

Set the work to be ornamented on a
pitch-block as if for repoussé. Carefully
scratch or draw the pattern upon the
metal. Place the work in front of you so
that the line of ornament is perpendicular
to yourself ; then holding the chisel between the thumb and first two fingers
(see fig. 201), with the head of the chisel
slanting away from you, drive it along the
line towards you, taking care that the cut
be not too deep or too shallow. Remove
the resulting curved chip of metal, and
then continue the cut until you have
carried the line as far as necessary (see figs.
202 and 203).

On examining the cut you will find
that the line is burred upon both sides.

The leaves should be cut by somewhat
broader chisels with edges slightly on the
slant.

322

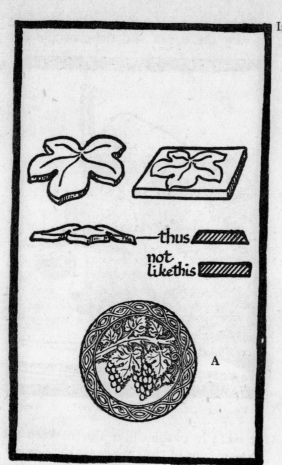

FIG. 200.

This slant enables the worker not only
to vary the depth and slope of the cut

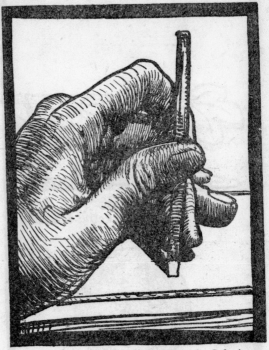

FIG. 201.—How to hold the Clutch for Inlaying.

at will; it enables him also to keep the
outline edge of the cut always the deepest.
This is necessary for the proper retention

324

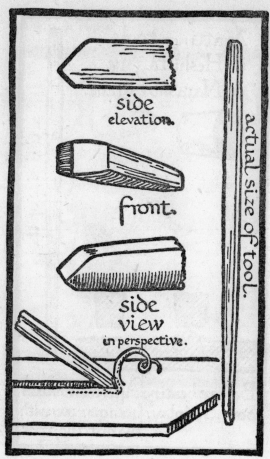

side
elevation.

front.

side
view
in perspective.

actual size of tool.

Fig. 202.

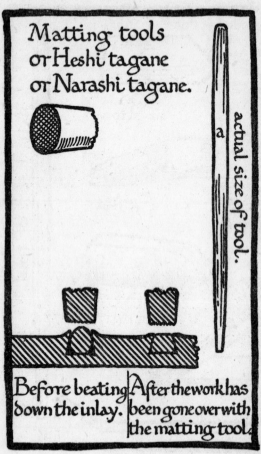

Matting tools
or Heshi tagane
or Narashi tagane.

actual size of tool.

a

Before beating
down the inlay.

After the work has
been gone over with
the matting tool.

FIG. 203.

of the inlaid metal. For larger spaces the ground within the outline is cut away and the floor of the recess levelled so as to have more room for the required thickness of metal.

When the pattern has in this way been completely outlined, get gold or silver wire of the exact width of the cut for the stem; anneal it, take a flat matting-tool (see fig. 203), insert the end of the wire in the channel, and give it a tap with the punch so as to fix it firmly in place. Then lay the wire in place along the cut and press it into position with the matting-tool along the sides of the cut without touching the wire. This drives down the burr raised up in the process of cutting, and produces the undercut necessary to hold the wire in place.

When inlaying broader wire it is well to have it oblong in section. One edge of the wire is then rubbed with the burnisher until a slight burr is produced

on each side thus.

The wire thus prepared is laid in the channel and fixed with the matting-tool as before.

327

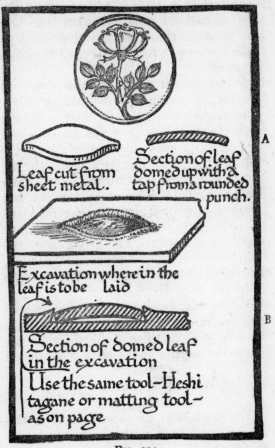

Leaf cut from
sheet metal.

Section of leaf
domed up with a
tap from a rounded
punch.

Excavation wherein the
leaf is to be laid

Section of domed leaf
in the excavation
Use the same tool—Heshi
tagane or matting tool—
as on page

A

B

FIG. 204.

Then with the same punch planish the wire down and make it even with the whole surface. The leaves are done in a similar way. The shapes are first of all cut from sheet-metal of the necessary thickness, and then filed to fit the excavation in the ground. Each leaf is then laid on a lead-block or on pitch and slightly bent (see A and B, fig. 204) or domed up with a tap by a rounded punch. Thus prepared it is dropped hollow side downwards into the excavation and tapped lightly with the small hammer. This spreads the metal out and at once makes it fit into the excavation, and when the burred edge of the latter is brought over by the matting and planishing punches it is held firmly in place.

The process is repeated until the pattern is complete. The surface is then cleaned with fine emery or sand paper, and stoned and polished in the usual way.

Simple Inlay—Another Method

The tools required for this are short, chisel-shaped tracers, curved and flat and square edged, of various sizes, a few

FIG. 205.—Method of Inlaying Wire.

matting-tools, and a few sharp cutting-chisels.

Suppose the pattern to be inlaid is something like that shown in the border of A, fig. 200, or in fig. 205. Having made the tracing from your drawing, transfer it with the pricker to the surface of the metal, which you have previously stoned and polished and fixed on the pitch-block. Take the fine wire you

FIG. 206.

propose to inlay, anneal it carefully, and select a bevelled tracing-tool with an edge like fig. 206 in side elevation, and trace the outline carefully, driving the punch in deeply. This done, take a flat-edged tracer (see fig. 207), the width of which is exactly the diameter of the wire to be inlaid, and go over the line already traced, beating down the ground to the required depth to receive the wire. The

FIG. 207.

FIG. 208.

section of the metal will now be as in fig. 208; that is, the last tracing will have left the ridges formed by the first tracer, while deepening and widening the channel.

331

At this point it is well to try if the wire will lie comfortably in the groove. If it does not, then go over the work with a very slightly broader tracer. Insert the wire, fix the end with a tap with the hammer or the matting-tool, bend the wire into its place with the fingers, drive it home with a boxwood punch, and trace lightly on either side of it with the matting-punch, so that the raised burr is driven down against the sides of the wire. Next beat down the wire

FIG. 209.

itself into the under-cut channel which the matting-tool has made (see fig. 209) by driving over the burred edges. The inlay is now secure, and the metal can be filed or made smooth with the emery-cloth, and then stoned and polished (see fig. 203).

Should the wire at any stage become springy after you have hammered it into its place, cut the springy portion out, re-anneal it, and repeat the process above described, deepening the channel if necessary.

Should you wish to have the wire inlay appear as if slightly raised above the

332

surface, you can do so by making a tool
like a planisher, but having a shallow
groove filed on the top surface. The
section of this groove (see fig. 210) should
be a quarter of the circumference of the
wire before inlaying. The edges of the
groove and the tool should be nicely
rounded and made smooth to the
touch with fine emery-cloth before
being used. You can now go over
the inlaid wire and drive down the
metal on either side, using the FIG. 210.
tool as you would a tracer. The outer
edges of the slight grooves resulting from
this can be removed with a planisher, or
they can be scraped off with the chisel
edge of the burnisher, or the ground can
be matted, pearled, or tooled in any way
you may select.

CHAPTER XL

Raised Inlay.

RAISED inlay is done as follows :—
Having made a perfectly clean drawing
of what you propose to make—let us suppose a circular silver panel for a buckle,
as in figs. 200, 204, 212c—take your silver,

333

actual size of tool.

'b', trace round the outline with these tools keeping the head of the tool inclined slightly inwards and under cut.

'a', outline scratched with a point.

A

Namekuri tagane

FIG. 211.

which should not be less than size 14, cut
out and dome up the shape, file the edge
clean and stone the surface until smooth.

Fix it on a pitch-block, taking special
care that the pitch shall be neither too
hard nor too soft, but so that it can be
easily indented with the nail when cold.

The composition used by Japanese
artists, and made from pine resin and
plaster, is better than the ordinary pitch
and plaster compound used in repoussé
work.

Fix the panel on the pitch, and having
made a tracing of the design, transfer it
by pricking round the outlines with a fine
point. This done, take your gold—fine
gold, twenty-two carat and sixteen carat
gold, the last two alloyed with fine silver
only for the leaves, the stems, and the
grapes—roll it out to about size 8, and
transfer carefully the drawings of the
leaves and grapes and stems to their
respective alloys, and cut round the outline carefully with a fine chisel on a steel
bench-stake or anvil.

File the shapes true with a fine needle-
file, giving each leaf a slight bevel (see
fig. 200), slightly dome each piece, and
bend it so that it will lie comfortably in

335

Fig. 212.

its place on the ground prepared. Then
with a point scratch the outline of that
leaf which is lowest in relief upon the
silver exactly in its place (see fig. 211).

This done, take a sharp tracer with
bevelled edge, like the enlarged drawing
(A, fig. 211), and trace round the outline,
keeping the head of the tool inclined
slightly inwards, so that the outline is
slightly undercut, and at the same time a
sharp edge or burr is raised all round.

This burr is a very important point, as
a great deal of the success of the work
depends upon it. When the outline is
clear, take the leaf or portion of a leaf
and lay it in the place to see if it fit the
outline (see fig. 212c). Correct it wherever necessary with great care. When the
leaf appears to fit, take a small chisel,
Kiritagane (see fig. 212B), and first go
round the outline, cutting away the
inner burr all round, and then remove
the ground to a depth just sufficient to
allow the leaf its proper projection. Fix
the leaf in place, and if it should not
exactly fit in every place, then take the
tracer and go round the outline, correcting
it where necessary and driving back the
metal, keeping always the burr and the

Y   337

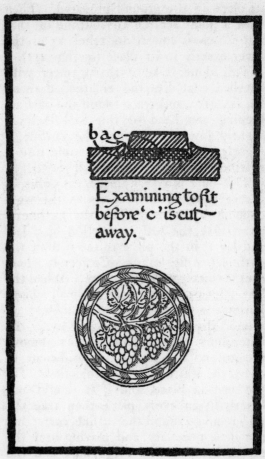

Examining to fit
before 'c' is cut
away.

Fig. 212c.

under-cutting clean and sharp. When
the leaf will just drop in and exactly fit,
lay it in place and give it a few taps
with the hammer to fix it. Take next
a small fine matting-tool and go carefully
round the outline, driving down the
raised burr against the edge of the leaf.
You will naturally fix the tips of the leaf
and the eyes of it first, then follow round
the contour in an orderly way.

This done completely, take fine chasing-
tools and model the surface and put in
the veins. This is best done by drawing
them first on the leaf with a fine brush
and Indian ink. This prevents any mis-
takes, and makes you more careful in your
modelling. Finish by going round the
outline with a fine bevelled tracer, and
then scrape the ground clean and bright
all round the leaf.

Having now got the first leaf firmly
fixed, take the form which comes next to
it. We will suppose this to be the lower
bunch of grapes (see figs. 200 and 212c).
Cut them out in the same way as the leaf,
and mark the outline clearly with the point
as before. This time you will have one
side of the form to be inlaid abutting on
the leaf just finished. In order to avoid

any injury to your leaf, you must take great care in outlining and cut cleanly, so as to get your form with as little disturbance as possible of the inlaid metal.

Cut out the ground within the outline as before, try the prepared shape frequently in place so that it may fit exactly, and inlay the grapes. When the metal is firmly fixed, outline the separate grapes with a bevelled tracer, model each one with a small planisher until you have the effect you desire.

Proceed in this way, never beginning any new leaf or form until the last is perfect, clean, clearly outlined and modelled, and the ground scraped clean and bright after each operation.

The remaining leaves and twigs will be done as above described. Always be mindful of the importance of testing the shapes in their places, making each fit exactly before beating down the burr.

The tendrils may require a somewhat different treatment. Outline the form with a single tracer line, and then take a flat, square-edged tracer like a narrow curved punch, and follow the curves, driving the metal down to form a flat-bottomed groove for the curve. Inlay the curved wire, which must be of the exact

340

width of the groove as before, driving the burr down against the curve with the fine matting-tool. Where the tendril passes over leaves or other forms, great care must be taken not to disturb them in the process, but if the work has been done well it will not be an easy matter to displace any portion of it.

Having carefully modelled the whole surface to your satisfaction, take a long scraper, one end of which is shaped as a chisel, the other as a bevelled scraper, and scrape down any irregularities which may be left in the modelling, refining where necessary with the graver, and finally stone and polish the ground with the scratch-brush, and burnish the grapes. The work may now be treated with sulphide of ammonia to darken it, or it may be subjected to any of the processes given in a subsequent chapter.

It will be obvious that the method of inlay will apply to almost any metals or alloys. A very wide range of coloured effects can be produced by the use of carefully chosen alloys, and these can be still further added to by using such alloys as take on brilliantly coloured patinas when pickled in an acid solution.

341

Raised Inlay Where there is a large amount of inlaid gold, fine silver may be plated with a thin sheet of gold, and used as if it were solid metal. The same may be done with the various alloys.

CHAPTER XLI

Damascene Work.

Damascene Work THE Japanese method of damascene work is, like all the work of that people, one of exquisite simplicity.

It, no less than incrustation work, depends for its success on two things. (1) On the careful preparation and whetting of the chisels used; (2) on the careful use of them when made.

The tools required are—1. A small, light, well-balanced tapping-hammer. 2. A chisel whetted for outlining. 3. Two or three chisels of varying sizes for hatching or roughing the ground of those portions to which the gold or silver leaf is to be applied. 4. A long, leaf-shaped burnisher with one end ground to a cutting-chisel edge. 5. Small corn-tongs. 6. A fine, long-haired brush and Indian ink for outlining the ornament upon the steel.

342

7. Thick gold-foil such as is used for enamelling. If this is not procurable, fine gold may be rolled down or hammered out to the required degree of thinness without very great difficulty.

In any case, fine gold or silver are the best for use. If, however, the gold be alloyed with only a very small quantity of silver, it is possible to make it serve, but the gain in gold is not compensated by the loss of time in making it stick to the ground. Alloys should therefore only

FIG. 213.

be used where contrast of colour is indispensable.

To prepare the tools, take some fine tool steel a little more than one-eighth square in section, and cut it into three-inch lengths. For the outlining chisel file up the blank as for a narrow planisher or a drill blank. There should, however, be a flat on one side only. This is to form the upper surface of the chisel. Bend the chisel slightly in the direction of the flatted surface (see figs. 211, 213), and set the tool on one side for hardening and

343

tempering. The chisels are filed up as for tracing-tools and the taper made curved on two sides (see Kiritagane, figs. 213 and 215). They must now be hardened and tempered. The whole success or failure of the work largely depends on the care with which this is done. Take one of the chisels, heat the end red-hot, have ready beneath the flame a pot of cold water; when the metal glows, dip the cutting end of the tool $\frac{3}{4}$ of an inch into the water for an instant only. Withdraw quickly and watch closely until the heat from the unchilled portion of the tool invades the chilled portion and turns the grey-white of the latter to a very pale straw-colour, then instantly chill the whole tool, and it is ready for whetting. The outlining chisel must now be whetted on a fine-grained Washita stone to the shape shown in figs. 213, 215. Great care must be taken to get the end of the tool absolutely true and symmetrical, or it will not be possible to cut a clean line with it. If the bevels on either side incline too much to right or left, the tool will err in the opposite direction. If the triangular bevel on the front face is too steep the tool will not cut properly, while if it is not steep

344

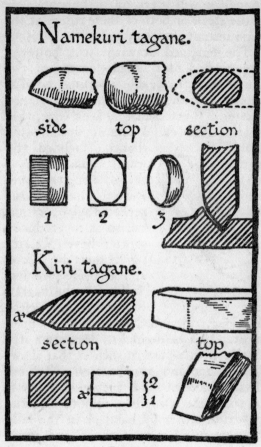

Namekuri tagane.

side   top   section

1   2   3

Kiri tagane.

section   top

FIG. 214.

enough it will break off or bury its nose
in the steel, or both of these things at the
same instant (figs. 213 and 214).

The enlarged drawings will, however,
give a good idea of the nature of this
simple but invaluable instrument. The
whetting of the chisels is a much simpler
matter. Whet each to a keen edge, then
holding the chisel almost upright but

FIG. 215.

slightly inclined to-
wards you, draw it
sharply along the stone.
Reverse the tool and
repeat the operation,
but so as to produce a
shorter bevel, *i.e.* the
stroke must be shorter
and the pressure less.
A glance at the diagram
will make this clear.

In using, this broad bevel is kept uppermost. If it be desired to decorate a steel
buckle with a pattern such as that shown
in figs. 200 and 204, proceed as follows.
Take a piece of mild sheet-steel, gauge 14
or 16, dome it slightly, remove the crust
of oxide either by hand or in the lathe
by cementing it to a chuck and grinding down the surface with emery-cloth.

346

The surface should be quite smooth and bright.

Fix the metal on a pitch-block or on a mass of pitch fixed on a stout piece of plank cut to a convenient size to handle, planed clean and smooth, and the angles taken off so that it is pleasant to touch. The pitch should be poured to form in the centre of this board a mass large enough to hold the metal firmly and also to raise it sufficiently high for convenience in working. Everything at this stage should be clear, bright, neat and attractive-looking. Much depends on this. Transfer your pattern or sketch it on the steel with the fine brush and Indian ink. A little ammonia spirit or methylated spirit in a rag on a bit of cotton-waste will remove all grease and make work with the brush more easy. Should the ink still refuse to lie, add a little oxgall, or rub a very little soap into the ink. Now take the outlining chisel, and holding it as described for inlay work, go all round the outline of the pattern chosen, holding the chisel in your left hand and driving it towards you.

When all is clearly and cleanly outlined, take the hammer and smaller-sized chisel,

347

and holding the head of it inclined
slightly away from you (see fig. 201), cover
the whole surface of the leaf with a close-
set series of cuts like those on a file. This
done, see that there is no inequality of
cutting anywhere on the surface, and repeat the operation with a series of cuts
at an angle of about 45° with the
last. The slope of the cuts themselves
must be in the same direction as the
first. If this work has been properly
done, the ground within the leaf will be
slightly higher than that outside. Take
a piece of gold-foil just large enough to
cover the leaf, lay it in place, and having
wetted the burnisher, hold the latter
between the thumb and finger of the
right hand with the end-half of it resting
against the palm of that hand and pressing
down on the burnishing portion with the
thumb of the left hand; go smoothly with
a slight rocking motion over the surface
of the gold, stroking it with firm pressure
from side to side rather in the direction
of the cuts, so that the tiny points of
steel may enter the thickness of the gold,
and then, being further pressed down,
may hold it firmly. The gold itself being
plastic is also by the same operation

348

forced into the interstices of the steel and
forms a key giving additional security.
The superfluity of gold beyond the leaf
outline is removed by using the chisel-
edge of the burnisher as a knife, cutting
the gold and at the same time pressing
it down into the groove formed by the
outline.

The same procedure is followed for the
remainder of the ornament.

Damascening can be done without outline, in which case the ground is roughened all over and the leaves and ornament cut to shape with graver or chisel.
Theophilus gives a method by which this
can be done mechanically on the lathe.
The student might find it interesting to
refer to this.

When all is done, you can either cover
the ground with a grain pattern by using
a fine pearl-tool or various mats formed
by different matting-tools. The surface
can be coloured or darkened to varying
tones of grey, from the pale colour of
the steel to intense purple-black, by the
use of strong or weak infusions of ordinary
tea, and leaving the work in the infusion
a time proportionate to the depth of
colour you wish to obtain. This colour,

349

when the work is dry, can be intensified
by the use of a little wax rubbed in with
a hard brush.

This method of damascening has many
applications. It can be used to decorate
repoussé work or carved work in iron or
steel, and is capable of producing the
most enchanting effects of richness with
a very little comparative labour; but
that labour must be applied with the
greatest concentration. To be effectual,
all work must be done with the edge of
the mind a little in advance of the tool.

CHAPTER XLII

Japanese Casting—How to Cast a Modelled Vase in Metal.

IN essentials the Japanese method is the
same as that described fully by Theophilus, but the former includes so many
refinements in application and improvements in material, that some account of
them may be useful. For all the information in this and most of that in the
succeeding chapter on Japanese metal-
colouring, I am indebted to Professor
T. Kobayashi of Tokyo.

350

How to Cast a Modelled Vase in Metal

First have ready to hand the following materials :—

Wax.—Prepare a sufficient quantity of modelling wax, made by melting one pound of Japanese pitch, or best Burgundy pitch, and one pound of best beeswax. Boil the pitch and then add the wax, and stir the mixture until the ingredients have become incorporated. It can be coloured by adding a little colouring matter if so desired. When required for use it should be kept in a bowl of warm water.

Clays for the Mould and the Core.—Special kinds of clay mixture will be required. The first is kami tsuchi, or paper clay. This is made of fine casting sand, Japanese paper, and ordinary potter's clay.

The paper used must be such as has a long fibre. Newspaper, or indeed any wood-pulp paper, is useless. Waste Japanese packing-paper can be obtained at any of the Japanese stores.

The casting sand must be well burnt to rid it of all organic impurities. The paper must be well soaked in water or boiled. If casting sand cannot be pro-

cured, finely powdered brick or burnt
clay may be used instead.

In very fine work powdered graphite or
powdered charcoal may be added to the
sand.

Mix the sand with the clay and then add
the Japanese paper, well soaked. Knead
the mixture well with the hands until
all the materials are so thoroughly incorporated that, on pulling a piece of the
clay apart, the separated surfaces appear
as if covered with a very fine down or
mould.

Test a piece by firing. If, after it has
been baked to redness, it should crack in
the furnace, there is too much clay. If
the paper is in excess it will be too brittle.

Tama tsuchi, a grade coarser than the
above, is made of chopped tow, sand, and
wet clay. The sand should be passed
through a sieve with meshes one-third of
a millimetre square, and the whole should,
as before, be thoroughly well mixed by
hand.

Tsuta tsuchi (chopped straw clay), the
coarsest grade, is made of straw chopped
into lengths, wet clay, and casting sand,
sifted through a sieve with half millimetre
meshes, and is mixed as before described.

Shigata tsuchi (or core clay).—Next the core clay will be required. This will be needed in two grades—shiage tsuchi, or finishing clay, a mixture of casting sand made pasty with clay alone; and shigata tsuchi, or core clay, made with clay, sand, and chopped straw.

Have all these ready in suitable boxes or receptacles so as to be ready at any instant.

The alloy of bronze should now be prepared. The mixture commonly used is—

Copper, 75 per cent. to 80 per cent. } 8 lbs.
Lead   25   „   to 28   „
Shirome .   .   .   .   .   3 ozs.

Shirome, which may be omitted, is a natural alloy, chiefly composed of antimony.

The above alloy must be very carefully prepared, as it is very difficult to make a eutectic alloy of copper and lead.

Melt the copper first, and when it is liquid add a little of the lead. Stir carefully with a dry stick, then add a little more, stirring continually. Then pour out into ingots, and when cool remelt and pour into ingots at least three times.

z

Making the Core for the Vase.—We may
now make the core. Take an iron rod
about one-eighth to one-quarter of an inch
in diameter, longer than the vase by
about two or three inches, and wind some
tightly twisted straw- or hay-rope tightly
round it. Dab the rope with clay water,
and then apply shigata tsuchi, or the core
clay, until you have a rough approxima-
tion to the shape of the vase. Next cut
a templet of sheet-iron to the profile of
the vase, turn the core against the templet
either by resting the projecting ends of
the iron rod on two wooden uprights
prepared for it, or by fixing the vase
upright on a board and making a revolving
trammel, such as plasterers use. When the
rough core shape is dry apply a thin coat
of finishing clay ; turn it into shape with
the templet, and repeat the process until
the contour is perfect all over.

When this is dry the wax should be
applied. Roll out the wax, previously
softened in hot water, on a smooth board
kept wetted. The wax should be rolled
out to the desired thickness of the metal
for the future vase.

With a warmed knife, cut it into strips
from half an inch to one inch wide,

354

according to the shape of the vase, narrow strips for quick curves and broader strips for flatter curves (see fig. 216), and cover the core with them. Smooth the wax all over with a warmed steel modelling tool, making good deficiencies wherever necessary.

Any decoration desired, incised or modelled, may now be added, always using the same kind of wax, and being careful to see that any applied modelling adheres well to the ground and that the junction between it and the ground is well filled up. If this precaution be neglected it may easily happen that a carefully modelled figure or dragon or plant may fail to come out in the metal because the points of attachment to the vase—which form the gates of access to the matrix of the applied modelling—have not been large enough to let the metal through them freely.

The bottom mouldings, or foot of the vase, should be carefully made, and when the whole model is complete, two or more wax rods, according to the size of the vase, four inches long by three-eighths of an inch diameter, or about as thick as the little finger, must be prepared and attached to the bottom of the vase (see fig. 216).

355

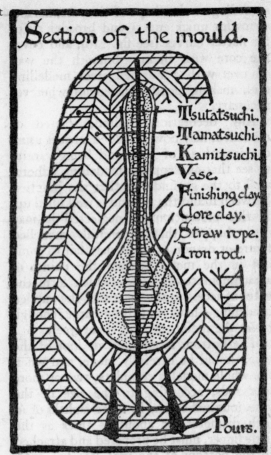

Section of the mould.

Itsutatsuchi.
Mamatsuchi.
Kamitsuchi.
Vase.
Finishing clay.
Core clay.
Straw rope.
Iron rod.

Pours.

FIG. 216.

It is well to make these a little thicker at the upper end, so that a funnel-shape is left in the mould when the wax has melted. Should there be any projections in the modelling, or any part which is detached at any point from the vase, slender rods of wax rolled out on the wetted board should be attached to these portions and led to, and beyond, the bottom of the vase, so that the air may be able to escape from the matrix as the metal enters it.

The mould should now be covered as thinly as possible with kami tsuchi (paper clay), the first clay mixture. The greatest care must be taken to ensure that this coat enters all the crevices, fills up all the hollows in the modelling, and is even in thickness all over.

When this coating has dried in the air, a second coating of the tamai tsuchi (or tow clay) must be applied more thickly, but still evenly, and allowed to dry. A third coating of tsuta tsuchi must then be added and the mould shaped up into a form that may easily be handled. The whole mould should now be allowed to dry for three or four days in the air, setting it in a place through which the wind can blow freely.

357

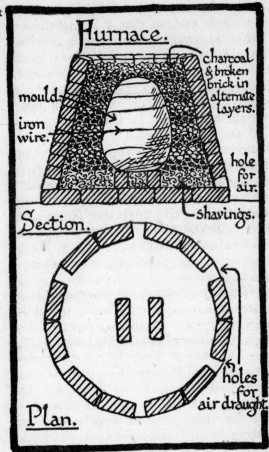

Furnace.

charcoal
& broken
brick in
alternate
layers.

mould.

iron
wire.

hole
for
air.

Section.

shavings.

Plan.

holes
for
air draught.

Fig. 217.

While the mould is drying you may prepare the furnace.

On a foundation of fire-bricks, laid side by side upon the ground, make a circle of brick, not less than six inches larger than the mould all round. From this circle omit four or five bricks to make air-inlets. In the centre of this, set two or three bricks on edge, to form a stand for the mould. On these, well bound round with stout iron wire, the mould is set, bottom upwards. Continue the enclosing wall above the top of the mould, taking care that the bricks break joint with each other and that the walls incline inwards (see fig. 217).

Set a layer of shavings on the floor of the furnace, then a layer of charcoal, or finely broken coke, after that a layer of bricks broken small. Layers of charcoal and brick follow one another in succession until the furnace is full to the top. Arranged in this way, the furnace burns smoothly, gradually, and evenly, and the mould is less likely to crack through the uneven distribution of heat.

When all is ready light the shavings at the bottom. In about twenty minutes steam will begin to issue from the mould,

359

and in about an hour the mould should be red hot.

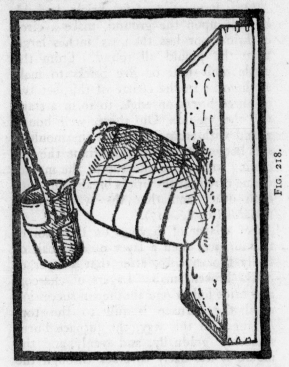

FIG. 218.

The temperature required is about 1100° Fahr., not more.

It will now be necessary to stop up the air-inlets and allow the fire to cool gradually. While the mould is cooling it will be well to melt the bronze in a large crucible, which can be done either in a gas furnace or in a similar furnace to that made for baking the mould. Keep a layer of crushed charcoal on the top of the molten metal to prevent undue oxidation. When the fire has cooled somewhat, but the mould is still at a red heat inside, remove it carefully with large tongs, and set it, mouths uppermost, on the ground, or on a bed of dry sand. The mould should now be made to incline slightly to one side, so that one pour, or gate, is at a lower level than the other, yet not so much that the mould will be likely to fall over (see fig. 218).

Take the crucible in the tongs, remove the scoria and charcoal from the surface of the molten metal, stir it to ensure complete mixture of the metals, and holding with other tongs a cloth thickly folded over and over to the lip of the crucible, pour the metal into the uppermost opening of the mould. Do this steadily, listening the while for any sounds of bubbling or disturbance within the mould. If noises are heard it means that air cannot escape quickly enough. If this

361

should happen, cease pouring for an instant. This may diminish the evil, but in any case the cast is likely to be defective, or at the best porous. When the mould is full, the bronze will run out at the lower pour or gate.

The mould may be left to cool for a while, but the cast must be removed before it is quite cold, or it may, by shrinking within the mould, become cracked, or portions of the modelling may detach themselves from the body of the vase.

When quite cool it can be pickled to remove the crust of oxide, and is then ready for chasing and finishing.

CHAPTER XLIII

A Method of Casting Natural Objects in any Metal.

NATURAL objects, such as fir cones, buds, beetles, lizards, snakes, or shellfish, anything which will resist pressure and is reducible to ash by heat, can be cast by the following method, which is an adaptation of that first described.

Take a quantity of tsuta tsuchi (chopped hay and clay) and make a foundation with it large enough to give a bearing surface

362

not less than $1\frac{1}{2}$ inches wide all round the object. On this foundation lay a thin layer of kami tsuchi (paper clay) after moistening the foundation layer, and press well down into the latter so that the two become incorporated.

Into this press the object to be cast. It should be embedded in the clay for a little more than half its thickness. Attach to the object two wax pours or runners for the ingress of the metal, and dust the foundation and the object with finely scraped bath-brick or fine moulding-sand or French chalk, so that the mould may separate easily into two halves when it is necessary to remove the remains of the object to be cast.

Remove all dust, sand, or parting powder from the object with a camel-hair brush, then cover all with a very thin layer of kami tsuchi (paper clay) well pressed down so that all the interstices of the model are filled up. Insert on either side wooden or plaster of Paris wedges as shown on the sketch (fig. 219). When the mould is nearly dry these can be removed, and when quite dry the resulting holes afford a means of prising the mould apart without damaging it unduly. Moisten with clay-water and

apply a layer of tsuta tsuchi. Dry the
mould in the air as before described, tie
up the mould with some iron binding-
wire, and heat it as before, but this time
so that the heat is above 1200°. The
carapace of crustacea, such as crabs,
crayfish, and lobsters, does not change its
composition until this heat is reached.
The mould when cool can be opened.
The ashes of the object forming the
pattern can be dusted out, unreduced
portions being picked out with a needle,
and when clean the mould may be tied
together with iron binding-wire, heated
red-hot again in the furnace and the
molten bronze poured in.

Should the object be so large that it
becomes necessary to cast it hollow, this
can be done after the mould has been
opened. Take core clay, press it in small
quantities at a time into the two halves
of the mould, so that the latter is not
injured by undue pressure. It will not
be necessary to do more than fill the
larger masses. The smaller portions can
be left solid. Join the two half impressions carefully with thick clay-water or
slip. Dry in the air, and then scrape
from this core a thickness of clay equi-

valent to the thickness desired for the
metal; lay it in place, support it with
little pieces of bronze of the required
thickness, and lay little pieces also on the
top of the core. Set the upper half of
the mould in place and tie the two
together with binding-wire, and proceed
as above described for the casting of the
vase.

CHAPTER XLIV

Japanese "Woodgrain" Metal.

VERY beautiful effects are produced by a
method akin to that used in producing
damascened steel.

To do this, several sheets of copper
will be required—one of pure copper, the
others having varying amounts of tin
alloy—a sheet of silver, and one of an alloy
of copper containing a slight percentage of
gold.

Lay the sheets together, having first
sprinkled each with fine silver solder
filings and borax; tie them together
securely with binding-wire, and heat on the
forge with the blow-pipe until the solder
flushes everywhere. Then take the re-

sulting slab of metal, hammer it well on a smooth anvil with a heavy planishing-hammer, and reheat with the blow-pipe until you see that the plates have all united into a solid mass. Then with a chisel gouge out circular pits or deep markings in the upper surface of the metal, so that you cut through two or three layers of the metal. Then take the planishing-hammer and beat the slab out or put it through the flatting-rolls until these pits disappear.

Featherings, mottlings, grainings of great variety can be produced in this way, or by bumping or beating out the metal from the back, and then grinding flat on the face. By use of the rolls you can of course reduce the composite sheets of metal to any desired thickness.

When the work made of these composite sheets of metal has been completed and polished, the various processes for producing patina act differently on the different metals, giving a mottled or grained effect.

A little thought will suggest many variations and applications of this fascinating method of surface decoration.

366

CHAPTER XLV

Patinas.—The art of artificially and yet permanently colouring the surfaces of metals has been brought by the Japanese to a very high pitch of perfection.

The following recipes can be relied on to produce beautiful results if ordinary care is exercised and the following precautions are taken.

First : All the ingredients must be very perfectly mixed.

Second : All the instruments used in handling the objects to be coloured must be of copper or wood. Iron or steel must never be used. Galvanic action ensues immediately and entirely changes the result.

Third : The objects to be coloured must be chemically clean and in some cases highly polished beforehand.

Fourth : If the solutions are used hot,

367

different results are produced from those which come when used cold.

Generally it may be observed that the best and richest colours are produced on cast metal. Being porous, the metal is more readily acted upon by the solution. In all hammered or chased work the colour comes more slowly.

When heating any bronze work, care should be taken not to overheat it. The result of overheating is to sweat the tin to the surface of the metal.[1] This not only makes the skin of the metal harder and more impenetrable, but it produces a whitish bloom upon it, which can only be removed with great difficulty. In addition to this inconvenience, the ordinary pickles for the production of patina will not act where there is an excess of tin. Inequality in the distribution of the alloy is one of the many causes of failure to obtain the expected colour.

[1] It may be mentioned that this peculiarity of bronze alloys was known and utilised in Egypt from the earliest times. Bronze tools which required an edge or a surface of hardened metal were regularly case-hardened by heating the implement until the tin sweated to and hardened the surface, leaving the interior more ductile and tenacious. When the work has been well done, even a steel file will hardly touch it.

368

Bronzing by the Boiling Process—The Foundation Colour.—The ingredients required for the foundation colour are to be mixed in the following proportions :

Copper sulphate . . .	5 ozs.
Japanese verdigris . . .	5 ozs.
Water	1 gallon.

This solution can be applied to copper, bronze, brass, and silver.

It gives to copper or brass a warm brown colour and to bronze a dark brown colour. The greater the proportion of lead in the alloy, the darker will be the resulting colour.

This solution once made keeps indefinitely. The older it is the better.

It has the further advantage that by slight changes in the proportions of the ingredients or by the addition of other chemicals different results can be obtained. A little excess of copper sulphate produces a deeper colour, which can be made still deeper by the smoking process to be described later. The addition of copper acetate or of vinegar gives the patina a bluish tinge if the surface of the metal has been roughened. Green colour is produced by the addition of copper carbonate.

The mixture chosen should be applied thus :

Clean the object well with a solution of cyanide of potassium, and attach a copper wire for convenience in handling. Put it in the solution, which should be cold. Heat the vessel on the charcoal for several minutes. Take it from the fire, allow it to cool, and then reboil several times. The first boilings never give good results.

Should you wish to produce the bluish patina above described, the surface of the object must be roughened by the use of a strong solution of sal-ammoniac, oxalic acid, copper sulphate, and calcium chloride in about equal proportions. To get a uniform patina of this colour takes much time and patience. After the object has been boiled several times, it should be put on one side, and wiped with a wet cotton cloth once a week, until you have succeeded in producing the effect you seek. The process may be extended over many weeks, months or even years.

A reddish patina can be given to iron and bronze objects by boiling them in tea, to which iron filings have been added. Any kind of tea will do ; the stronger the better. The colour of the patina may afterwards be darkened by wiping the object with a rag, on which a little oil has been placed. Any excess of oil simply makes dark blots of colour difficult to remove.

A greyish colour can be given to bronze by the use of a dipping or washing mixture, composed of the following ingredients :—

Copper sulphate . . .	1 oz.
Common salt	$\frac{1}{20}$th of an oz.
Water	$\frac{1}{4}$ oz.

The metal must be chemically clean, and after each application should be allowed to dry, then well washed with warm water. This routine should be followed until the colour is satisfactory.

A dark green patina for bronze is produced as follows :—

Copper nitrate . . .	48 grains.
Sal-ammoniac	48 grains.
Calcium chloride . . .	20 grains.
Copper sulphate . . .	10 grains.
Oxalic acid	10 grains.
Water	4 fluid ozs.

More sal-ammoniac and copper sulphate make the colour darker.

If a bright green patina be desired, omit the copper sulphate and the oxalic acid.

Having carefully cleaned the object, apply several coats at intervals of a day. When the colour seems even and pleasant brush the surface with a dry brush. Do this several times, day after day, until you have the colour you desire. The patina may then be fixed by brushing with a little beeswax, rubbed on with a hard brush. This, however, makes the colour many shades darker ; and should any change be desired, the wax can only be removed with great difficulty by petrol or spirit of wine.

A grey colour on silver is obtained by using :—

Platinum chloride	. . .	10 grains.
Tincture of iron	. . .	1 fluid oz.

Clean the metal perfectly from grease and dirt. (Carbon bisulphide, applied with a soft brush, will give a bright clean surface to silver.) Apply the solution with a soft camel-hair brush, and when dry brush it over with a dry camel-hair brush. This gives a beautiful grey patina which is useful for medals and small objects in silver, whether beaten up or chased or produced in a die.

A dark blue colour on silver is produced by a mixture of :—

Quicklime	2 ozs.
Flowers of sulphur	¼ oz.
Water	6 ozs.

The work should be cleaned, warmed, and dipped in the mixture. The hotter the water, the quicker the action of the pickle. A similar result is produced by heating the pickle.

When the required depth of colour has been obtained, withdraw the work swiftly and wash well in warm water to remove the pickle and prevent the darkening process from going too far.

The Smoking Process.—Any of the colouring processes mentioned may be supplemented by the smoking process, which consists in the exposure of the object to the smoke and flame of a fire of pine needles, resinous shavings, or rice straw. Should the material used give insufficient smoke, add a little oil to the fire. When the colour appears dark enough, polish by rubbing gently with a soft cotton cloth. This removes any excess of soot and gives a beautifully lustrous surface. The process may be

373

used with effect for almost any metal with the exception of gold.

The fumes of burning flowers of sulphur give a beautiful brownish patina to silver, and a purplish colour to low carat gold. 9 carat, 12 carat, and 15 carat are most easily affected. Higher grades of gold remain unchanged.

The Painting Process.—This is a method by which the chemicals necessary for the production of patina and colour are applied very gradually by the paint-brush.

Bronze, iron, or steel objects can be coloured by the use of a solution prepared as follows :—

Take small pieces of bright iron, heat them to straw colour, then drop them into cold vinegar. This mixture should be left to mature for a long time. The longer it is kept the better it becomes.

Iron and steel treated with this solution become dark grey or black, according to the length of the process, the age, and the strength of the solution. Bronze is given a reddish colour.

The object to be coloured should be slightly heated, the solution painted on, then wiped off with a cotton rag. Repeat the operation several times until the

374

required colour has been obtained. The colour of iron or steel objects is greatly improved by heating them and rubbing them all over with an old silk rag. The metal should be just hot enough to singe the silk a light brown. The oil in the silk fibre is the active agent in the process.

A greenish patina of varying quality may be given to brass, bronze, and copper, and a pleasant warm, dark colour to silver, by the use of the pickle made as follows. Take of

Sal-ammoniac	. . .	$\frac{1}{20}$th of an oz.
Common salt	. . .	$\frac{1}{30}$th of an oz.
Water	.	5 fluid ozs.

Leave the mixture to dissolve until it is clear, then decant for use. Warm the article, brush on the mixture with a soft camel-hair brush—an ordinary sky brush used for water-colour painting will serve the purpose. After a moment, wipe the object dry with a soft cotton cloth. Repeat the operation of warming, painting, and wiping about twenty or thirty times. Little or no result will be apparent until the sixth or seventh repetition.

375

A very beautiful deep colour for bronze is also produced by the following :—

Copper sulphate	.	.	.	1 oz.
Japanese verdigris	.	.	.	1 oz.
Water	.	.	.	5 fluid ozs.
Sal-ammoniac	.	.	.	$\frac{1}{2}$ oz.

Mix the whole to a paste by grinding all the ingredients together in a mortar, adding water when the mixture has been ground quite fine.

Paint the object with the paste ; let it dry and remain for a day. Repeat for three or four days, then brush the object well. Afterwards wipe at intervals with a wet cotton rag. In about a month the colouring should be complete and may be fixed by wax, as before described. In Japanese workshops the process is continued on special pieces of bronze for many months, even years.

A more vivid green can be produced by using vinegar instead of water in the above recipe.

The Heating Process.—Heat the object until it is just red hot, then swiftly plunge it into boiling water. The metal must be red hot and the water must be boiling, or the resulting colour will be imperfect.

376

Copper treated in this way, after being highly polished, becomes deep crimson. Bronze takes on a deep red patina.

The purer the copper, the more brilliant the colour. The evenness of the patina depends on the even distribution of the heat over the surface of the object. For this reason it is well, where possible, to use a muffle furnace.

Other Recipes and Colouring Methods for Bronze Work.[1]—No. 1.   Cover the bronze with a mixture of ground horse-radish and vinegar.   Leave it on and keep it sprinkled with vinegar for some days.   Then wash with water under a tap.   Afterwards wipe at intervals with a wet cotton rag, until the desired evenness of colour has been obtained.

No. 2.

Strong vinegar	$\frac{1}{2}$ pint.
Chloride of ammonium . . .	$\frac{1}{4}$ oz.
Liquid ammonia	$\frac{1}{2}$ oz.
Common salt	$\frac{1}{4}$ oz.

Warm the metal and brush over the surface, repeating the operation after each coat has dried.   This gives what is called the antique green of bronze.

[1] From Spon's "Workshop Receipts," 1904.

377

No. 3.

Verdigris.	. . . . .	5 ozs.
Muriate of ammonia	. . .	5 ozs.
Strong vinegar	. . . .	½ fluid oz.

Mix the verdigris and ammonia by pulverising in a mortar. To this add sufficient vinegar to make a paste. Put this in a copper vessel with a pint of water and boil for thirty minutes. When cool, set on one side until the liquid clears. Then decant the clear portion and bottle for use.

Warm the bronze, paint the mixture with a brush, wipe off with a soft brush, and repeat until the colour is satisfactory.

No. 4. Mix

Powdered hæmatite	. . .	5 parts
Powdered plumbago	. . .	8 parts

to a paste with spirit of wine. Apply with a soft brush and leave it for some hours until quite dry. Brush off and polish with a fairly stiff, clean brush. The tint may be varied by altering the proportions at will.

This is not a pickle, nor, strictly speaking, a patina, but a colour.

No. 5. Black bronze patina is produced by the application of sulphate of am-

378

monium and water to the warmed surface of the metal. When the first wash is dry, cleanse the surface with hot water and repeat the application and the washing of the solution until the desired result has been obtained.

No. 6. For reddish bronze colouring, take of

Plumbago	.	.	.	.	.	1 oz.
Sienna earth	.	.	.	.	.	2 ozs.
Jeweller's rouge	.	.	.	.	.	$\frac{1}{2}$ oz.

Add a few drops of hydrosulphate of ammonium and water to make a paste, and apply as in No. 4.

No. 7. A purplish colour is obtained by applying to the warm metal a mixture of jeweller's rouge, crocus, and hydrosulphate of ammonia worked up into a paste. Brush off when dry, and repeat the operation until the tint is as you would wish. Leave it for a few days, then brush and polish as before described, with a hand-brush and a little wax.

No. 8. For a greenish patina, take of

Chromate of lead	.	.	.	.	2 ozs.
Prussian blue	.	.	.	.	2 ozs.
Plumbago	.	.	.	.	$\frac{1}{4}$ lb.
Sienna earth	.	.	.	.	$\frac{1}{4}$ lb.
Carmine lake	.	.	.	.	$\frac{1}{4}$ oz.

379

Add enough water to form a paste, afterwards mix with a little hydrosulphate of ammonia, and apply with a brush. Leave the coat to dry, and then brush off and repeat the process until the colour is as you wish.

These processes, 6, 7, and 8, combine the patina and actual colouring matter, and are, therefore, more permanent than No. 4.

CHAPTER XLVI

Japanese Metal Working.

By Prof. UNNO BISEI, of the Fine Art College, Tokyo.

A lecture delivered to the students of the Central School of Arts and Crafts.

IN attempting these demonstrations I feel somewhat diffident, particularly as I am to work before such advanced instructors and craftsmen, because we, as a nation, have been much influenced by European art and that of other civilised countries, particularly in the direction of metal working. However, since I have visited Europe and America, and have

380

been able to inspect and compare the
metal work exhibited at three universal
exhibitions, the importance of European
art has been brought home to me. I did
not, however, in either of the exhibitions,
or in my travels, see such imaginative
work as ours, especially where a combination of different metals is utilised to give
colour effects; although I must admit
that European arts are—not only in
painting and sculpture, but in other
departments—perfectly truthful in their
realistic beauty of form.

Japanese metal work made remarkable
progress during the period when bows and
arrows were instruments of warfare in
Japan—long before the introduction of
the gun.

The sword was especially richly ornamented with precious stones, and engraven
and damascened with gold—such as in
the examples you may see in the museums
and in the fine art palace of the Japan-
British exhibition.

The work was held in such esteem, and
indeed respect, that the sword was recog-
nised as a part of the Soul of the Samurai
—or Knight. The finest examples are of
the middle period of Ashikaga, 1338–1573,

reaching the most beautiful results in the Toyotomi period, A.D. 1583–1603, and the Tokugawa period, A.D. 1603–1867.

But two hundred years after the gun and revolver were imported from Europe, the decorative art of the metal worker on armour and arms began to decay, while on the other hand the production of metal work for decorative purposes increased, and, as statistics show, to a very considerable extent.

Japanese craftsmen in metals generally select the following metals for colour combinations:—Gold, silver, copper, brass, iron, Shibuichi, Shakudō.

The following are the methods of decoration in more general use in Japan.

1. KATAKIRIBORI.

   Engraving and reproducing the movement of brush-work.

2. HIRA-ZOGWAN.

   The inlaying of an object with different metals; for instance, to work a flower one uses gold for petals, copper for trunk, Shibuichi for leaves, &c. (See Chapter XLVI.)

3. TAKA-ZOGWAN.

   This is somewhat the same as Hira-Zogwan, but inlaid in relief. (See Chapter XL.)

4. UKIBORI.

   i.e. Chasing.

382

It is necessary to emphasise the importance of special alloys and the colours obtainable, more particularly as we have such a large number of alloys. For instance, there are no less than seventy different alloys for bronze, but of these about thirty are used at the present time. That number is, of course, beyond demonstration under present circumstances. Such a large number of alloys being used, you can well understand that there are also a considerable number of colouring solutions; but I am sure, with your ability and the small insight I am able to give you into our methods, you will be able to get satisfactory results such as the French are now managing, as may be seen in the work shown at the salons, and other exhibitions in Paris; the Japanese methods of alloy and colouring, as used in modern French metal work, being introduced by Monsieur Lucien Gaillet, to whom I had the pleasure of giving instruction in the work.

The alloy most generally used is that called " Shibuichi " :—

Copper . . . . . . 100 parts		
	(1) (2) (3) (4)	
Silver . . . 30, 40, 50, 60, or 70 parts		

The colour of the Shibuichi more

383

generally used is grey of a soft and pleasing tone, but you can make it dark or light, according to the proportion of your alloys. For instance, you wish to make a tree in flower, the petals of which may be made in gold if you wish them to be yellow, or silver if you wish them to be white. The leaves are to be in Shibuichi and of different colours, so you would make up your different grades of Shibuichi according to the quantity of silver employed, 1 to 4.

To make a darker Shibuichi, that which is called " Kuro-Shibuichi " in Japanese, is composed as follows :—

Shakudō	10 parts
Silver	3 or 4 parts

The methods of melting in order to produce Shibuichi is one which is simple after experience, but which requires considerable care. If the two alloys are melted at the same time you will not get the general Shibuichi colour, with fine spots showing grey grain—composed of silver and copper—like a pear skin, but, on the other hand, if the two metals are melted together, they will become somewhat darker and less of the nature of

384

Shibuichi, because the molecules of silver will have mixed too much with the copper.

Now, the first stage in the production of Shibuichi is to melt the copper as usual, and when it is quite melted put the silver in (sheet, or grain, or wire), and watch that it is not too much melted to mix. When this is done, pour into an oiled iron pot (the quantity of oil, rape-seed, about half, according to the size of the pot).

There is another way to mix the melting metals, viz. by taking a pot large enough for the quantity of metal, covering it with a common, but strong, cloth of a muslin-like nature (not too tightly stretched, so as to enable the metal to sink through), place it in hot water—just hot enough to put the fingers in—and then pour the metal through the cloth into the receptacle. This gives almost the same result, but it will probably bring a much softer and finer surface.

| Copper | . | . | 100 parts |
| Gold . | | . | 3, 4, 5, or 6 parts |

Shakudo.—The most common Shakudō colour is black, as you have seen, but it can be made in different colours, which gives an effect to the alloys.[1]   One which varies according to the paveture used from a colour somewhat similar to violet or dark violet is composed of 100 parts of copper and 10 parts of gold. If the gold is increased up to 20 parts, that is, 20 parts to 100 parts of copper, the metal becomes an exceedingly delightful colour, something like a deep plum-like bloom on the violet.

Colouring.—A useful colouring solution is composed of

> Verdigris, 1 dram (apothecaries' weight) ½ oz.
> Sulphate of copper, 1 scruple (apothecaries' weight) 1 dram (less).
> Water, 1 gallon or less.

Grind the medium and boil it with water, place the work in the solution, keep it moving, and examine it by taking it out occasionally. The time occupied in the colouring depends on the size and thickness of the object, but it generally occupies from 10 to 30 minutes, the time taken being according to your idea of what you consider a satisfactory result.

A copper sieve would be the best to use in placing in or lifting work out of the pan, or the work may be, if possible, suspended on a silver wire or wires, care being

[1] Used in the subsequent process of incrustation.

taken to keep the object on the move while in the solution.

It is important that you should avoid any kind of grease or oil, and the work should be thoroughly polished. Before starting work you should wash your hands well with soap, so as to keep the work clean and as free from grease as you can. The pan or utensil you use for the process of colouring should be either of china or copper, and not used for any other kind of metal or purpose. The following is a special preparation for the colouring of violet Shakudō :—

Sulphate of copper, 1 dram or less (apothecaries' weight) ½ oz.

Salt, ⅓ scruple (apothecaries' weight) ¼ dram.

Water, ½ ordinary glass or tumbler.

Boil the medium, then put the work into it, and take it in and out until you are satisfied with the colour.

Fig. 219 (*see page* 363).

387

FIG. 220.

CHAPTER XLVII

Egyptian and Oriental Methods.

I am indebted for most of the material in the following chapter to the researches of M. E. Vernier, whose admirable book on Egyptian jewellery and goldsmiths' work is a mine of precious information. The illustrations are an inexhaustible source of inspiration, and one is everywhere conscious in the text of an acute intelligence which illumines all it touches. My sincere thanks are due to M. E. Vernier for permission to use the blocks from which many of the diagrams illustrating this chapter have been made.

Egyptian and Oriental Methods

In all essentials the goldsmiths' craft is the same to-day as it was thousands of years ago. So-called developments and improvements will be found on examination to resolve themselves into appliances for saving labour or material; the craft itself is untouched by them, the craftsman

388

independent of them. The necessary, indispensable tools are singularly few and simple in character, and differ little wherever they are found. The stock-in-trade of the Egyptian, Hindoo, Arab, or Navajo gold- and silver-smiths might be used by each indifferently. With each workman the result is personal, the outcome of acquired and hereditary skill, a manifestation of the racial spirit, the expression of the underlying unity. This is everywhere a characteristic of supreme art.

With a little oil, some brushes, a few coloured earths, a length of coarse linen, and Millet, we have the Angelus.

With a few pebbles, some gold dust washed from some torrent bed, a few crucibles of clay and a reed from the Nile, the Egyptian mind produced the rings and scarabs and ouches which enrich the tombs of the Pharaohs. His tools lay everywhere to hand. He had but to select them. A large, smooth pebble or boulder for an anvil; smaller pebbles of varying forms and sizes served for hammers. A flake of flint took the place of shears. His furnace was built of clay and pebbles. A reed, tipped with a nozzle of clay, formed his

389

blow-pipe. From the river beds and the
desert he sought sapphires and sardonyx
and carnelians and jasper, shaped them
on grit stones and polished them with
powder, ground and crushed from the
emery nodules fished from the bed of
the Nile.

Refining these methods, he ground
precious stones into flat plates, and with
copper and bronze drills, smeared with
oil and emery, pierced them with holes
and shaped them into rings and bracelets,
or carved them into seals and pendants and
scarabs. All the arts seem to have their
germ in the art of the lapidary.

There is little doubt that the draw-plate
had its origin in the practice of drilling
holes in stone plaques, in order to pierce
out the centres of rings and bracelets, and
that the first draw-plates were made from
hard stone (see fig. 221). The ruby and
sapphire or diamond plate of the modern
jeweller repeats elaborately, but without
greatly increased efficiency, the primitive
invention. It may be said that of course
things can be done in these ways, but that
they need more time and patience than the
modern artist can afford to bestow on his
work. This may be so. But it may be

390

FIGS. 222 and 223.—Stone Moulds and Impressions in thin Metal.

From the Museum at Cairo.

See page 393.

questioned whether, after all, the time spent was so very long.

As Otis Mason in his admirable book, "The Origins of Invention,"[1] says: "A great deal that has been written about primitive industries is wide of the mark because the writer has failed to take into

Fig. 221.

account what may be called the knack of the age, or the tribe, or the particular method.

"He has described it as clumsy, and said that he could not for the life of him imagine how people could get along with such appliances. But they did. You

[1] "The Origins of Invention," by Otis T. Mason. Walter Scott, Paternoster Square.

391

will see a professional ethnologist sweating for hours to get a spark of fire with two sticks. The savage will do it for him in as many seconds.

"By-and-by the former acquires the knack, and then his trouble vanishes. . . . Mr. Joseph D. Macguire fabricates an ordinary grooved avec or celt in less than fifty hours, and a grooved jade avec from an entirely rough spall in less than one hundred hours. . . . Every one who reads this will recall examples of this deftness—and there is no doubt that this is the quality which in the higher pursuits of life we call genius."

In this, as in all work, much depends on that special prophetic gift possessed by every artist, and by every one in some degree, of knowing just how a given piece of work may be executed.

It is evident, however, that skill in lapidary work preceded that in metal work or goldsmithing, and that the experience of the workman in handling the more untractable material suggested many ways of dealing with the kindlier metals. The practice of beating out the gold ingots or nuggets into metal sheets, the readiness with which the thinning metal adapted itself to all the irregularities of hammer and anvil, giving imprints of all the flaws, early suggested the use of the swage and the hollow mould, of stone first, of metal later.

The idea soon developed, and fig. 222 shows two sides of a stone mould in each of which many varied patterns are sunk. Fig. 223 shows the forms produced when the metal has been impressed within the mould. This method, universally practised since, is of the greatest use when numbers of any one pattern are required, and has a further application which is perhaps less known.

In cases in which it is necessary to carry out in repoussé any complex form, or one in very high relief, the raising can be done by beating the sheet-metal into a reverse mould in bronze or iron cast from the matrix of a preliminary model, by means of wooden mallets and punches. The work then annealed and filled with pitch can be carried to any desired degree of finish with the greatest ease. The worker, moreover, knowing that the mould is always there, and that the form if lost temporarily can easily be regained, is given a freedom and confidence which he might otherwise lack. He need not fear to try experiments with his work. There is little doubt that this method was known to the Egyptians from the earliest times. The hawk-head shown in fig. 224 was in all probability first embossed by this means, and afterwards finished by

Fig. 224.

chasing, with tools in all essentials the same as those employed to-day, but made of bronze.

A reference to fig. 225 shows that the art of incrustation or inlay was also one of those practised, if not invented, by the

394

FIG. 225.—Bronze Hawk inlaid with Gold.
From the Museum at Cairo.

Egyptian craftsmen. The methods, even in those early times, were those everywhere in use at the present time in the East, and have been fully described in the chapter on Japanese inlay.

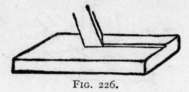

FIG. 226.

A few interesting details of the procedure adopted in the decoration of iron objects are given by M. Emile Vernier.

Objects in iron may be incrusted in the following way. Having traced the line to be followed on the metal, take a chisel with a single bevel, and holding it inclined sideways (fig. 226), cut a deep channel along

FIG. 227.   FIG. 228.

this line. Repeat the operation in the reverse way. This done, you have instead of a line a channel with a swallow-tail section (fig. 227).

The edges of the resulting burr raised

395

on each side of the channel are then cut
into teeth with the same chisel held aslant
(fig. 228), and the wire, carefully annealed,
is laid in the channel, and beaten in with

Fig. 229.

a slightly rounded punch or planisher
(figs. 229, 230). Grains or dots are inserted
by the following method. Take a graver
(whetted but not set) and make, at the
point to be decorated by the dot, a quad-
rangular cavity by holding the graver
slantwise and driving it sharply downwards

Fig. 230.

four times (see fig. 231), each cut making
a right angle with the preceding, and
the four together making a square.
This, if properly done, leaves a cavity
396

made of four juxtaposed triangular
pyramidal cavities (fig. 232), one side of
each of these pyramidal
cavities being bordered
by a burr, raised by
the flat side of the
graver. A grain of the
metal of suitable size

FIG. 231.

is now inserted in this cavity, and driven

FIG. 232.

inwards by a smart tap of the hammer
or a hollow-faced punch (see fig. 233).

397

This grain can now be driven home, the pointed burrs enter the grain of metal,

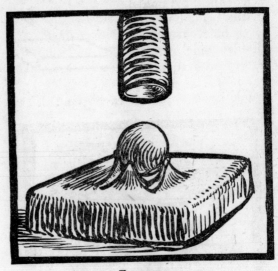

FIG. 233.

close over within its substance, and hold it securely in position (fig. 234).

FIG. 234.

The same methods are in use for brass, bronze, and silver, the only difference in the technique being that, owing to the softness of the ground

metal, the grooves must be made deeper.
Fig. 235 shows an inlaid bracelet from the
collection in the Museum at Cairo.

Another method of decoration, allied
to both incrustation and enamelling, is
that of niello work, a specimen of which
is illustrated in figs. 236 and 236 A. This

Fig. 235.

decoration, although undoubtedly of niello,
differs from the ordinary kind in the fact
that the ornament of precious metal has
been, as it were, embedded in a field of
niello. M. Vernier suggests that the units
of decoration were prepared from cloison

wire, laid on the surface of the niello and
then pressed into it by a slab of metal
sufficiently hot to melt the niello and
secure its attachment to the cloisons.
This may be the case, but no formula for
niello with which I am acquainted is
sufficiently fusible to permit of this. It
is quite possible to produce the same
result by laying the cloisons in the channel
prepared, filling up the space with niello,
and afterwards heating the whole until
the latter fuses. In any case, the process
employed in the decoration of the dagger
illustrated is capable of producing results
of great beauty.

Though the skill and inventiveness of
the Egyptian workman is shown in every
branch of craft, yet in few are the results
more remarkable than in the art of metal-
casting in sand. The methods employed
are those now universally in use, and
differ little, if at all (see fig. 220 at the
head of the chapter), from those already
described in the chapter on Casting.
Other methods, however, in constant use
by the Egyptian worker and still used by
primitive craftsmen are less employed
than they deserve. When several replicas
of a given pattern are required, the form

400

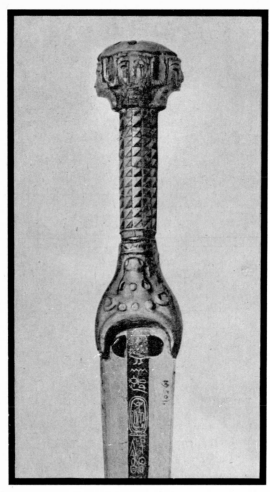

FIG. 236.—Egyptian Inlaid Dagger.

From the Museum at Cairo.

See also Fig. 236A facing page 416.

may be excavated in reverse in slate, serpentine, or steatite. In the counter-half the channels for the metal and the necessary air-vents and registers are provided. With proper care these moulds last a long time and more than pay for the trouble of making.

A piece-mould for casting rings is illustrated in fig. 237 (see plates facing page 408). Tapering hollows semicircular in section were excavated in the faces of two blocks of steatite. Register pins were formed on one half and corresponding cavities on the other. A base-block with register pins was next prepared, and on the block the sinkings and the designs for the chatons were cut in intaglio (fig. 240, see plates facing page 408). In the tapering hollows the sinkings for the ring shanks were engraved and the gates and vents and leads adjusted in the adjacent faces of these two portions of the mould. This done, a taper shaft of steatite or baked fire-clay was fitted to the taper hollow, and the mould, when tied together, was complete. Blanks for discs, pendants, or bangles were cast by a similar method. Fig. 238 shows a mould in serpentine used for this purpose, from the collection in Cairo. Fig. 239 shows the mould for a

2 C

platter, also in serpentine, proving the
adaptability of the method to larger work
than jewellery.

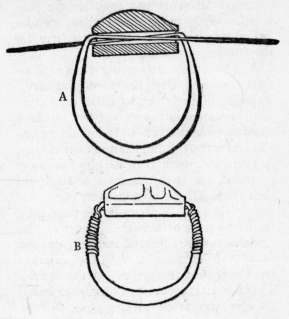

Fig. 241.

In whatever branch of art or craft we
examine we seem to find that the Egyptian
craftsman invented everything or knew it
always. With his swages for hollow brace-

lets, his moulds and stamps and dies for embossing, his fine cylindrical drills for hard stones and pearls, his filigree, inlaid

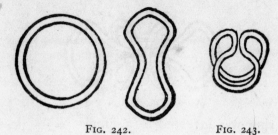

FIG. 242.   FIG. 243.

stonework and enamels, engraving, re-poussé, incrustation and lapidary work, nothing seemed impossible to his firm will and sweet intelligence.

Fig. 241 shows the earliest form of

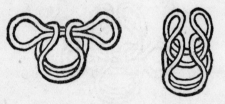

FIG. 244.

Egyptian ring, a scarab mounted as a taper gold wire. The whole fixing being simply done by passing the tapered ends

403

through to the hole in the scarab and winding them round the shank.

It seems evident from this that the

FIG. 245.

ring was invented as a simple means of carrying and using the signet.

Figs. 242 to 247 show an early method of making a cord chain, and from these the method can be followed without the necessity of any description.

In all the range of art there is no work

FIG. 246.

at once so happily impossible of imitation, and yet so full of precious suggestion and help for the hungry mind.

404

Happily for us, the methods and even Egyptian, and Oriental Methods the types of apparatus used in Egypt still survive throughout the East, indeed are to be found amongst the primitive workers all over the world. Opportunities for the study of these methods have from time to time been given by the exhibitions of native crafts organised at Earl's

FIG. 247.

Court and Shepherd's Bush, and at the present time by a more than usually interesting assemblage of Eastern craftsmen to be found working at the Coronation Exhibition.

Few things are more inspiring than the sight of the inborn skill of the Oriental as he sits at work : unhasting, unresting, his

405

attention utterly absorbed in his task; the fire of his mind burning on the point of his tool.

With almost equal wonder we regard his apparatus, and with a delicious shock of familiarity recognise things figured in missals and papyri and on the walls of tombs, or perchance described in manuscripts whose purport we have till now but incompletely grasped.[1]

The directions of the old lapidaries and gem engravers, the instructions written in "The Book of Divers Arts," are continually illustrated as we study the simple bowlathe of the Indian turner and the wheel of the gem-cutter, and the rudimentary apparatus of the goldsmith.

The sight of the real things gives continual testimony to the fidelity and utter singleness of purpose of that craftsman whose work was religion and who called himself Theophilus.

Fig. 248 will show better than many words the apparatus described often by Theophilus under the name of the "Turn." It could be erected for a few pence, and is one which every boy might well be encouraged to make and use. It consists

[1] See Plates facing page 416.

of two posts either driven into the ground or fixed to a bench, and a long bar of iron on which is fixed the object to be turned, and a cylinder of wood to give leverage and hold for the string of a bow or for a cord to be coiled round. Each end of the cord being pulled alternately by an assistant, the spindle is made to rotate so that the object can be turned.

Fig. 249 shows the lap used by the Indian gem-cutter for shaping, faceting, and polishing precious stones. Nothing could well be more simple nor, within its limits, more effective.

The wheel is an adaptation of the bow-drill, and consists of a disc of bronze or a composition of shellac and emery on a long pivot supported by two uprights. The length of the spindle between the supports and the disc is sufficient to allow the gut to be coiled round it and to give free play to the movement of the bow. A short cylinder of hard wood about $3\frac{1}{2}$ inches in diameter and $4\frac{1}{2}$ to 5 inches long is fixed on the spindle and acts as the pulley.

The rotation is not continuous but alternate, and the stone fixed in the cement-stick, as described on page 241, is held to the upper and lower halves of the

407

wheel alternately. With this primitive
apparatus both cabochon and faceted
stones can be cut. The latter naturally
have not the flawless regularity of the
machine-made gem, but are perhaps not
less attractive on that account.

The illustrations in fig. 250 show a
Sinhalese chaser at work. Here again
tools and methods are of the utmost
simplicity. A lump of pitch, a block of
wood, a hammer, a few simple punches, a
pair of pliers and a length of bamboo for
a blow-pipe form the whole outfit.

The pattern, though complex, has grown
by a process of simple addition, and, because they have learnt from their teachers
as those learned—by eye-memory—it de-
velops upon the plate as it were by a
simple act of will following the lines of
some unseen original.

They produce nearly all their effects by
outlining, then beating down the ground
with plain or mat tools. Any further
enrichment of the form, the tracing of
veins, fur, feathers, and features, is done
by the skilful use of variously shaped
punches.

For the elaborate, realistic modelling
sought by western craftsmen, an elabora-

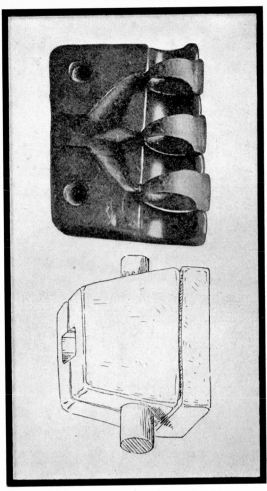

FIG. 237.—Steatite Mould for Casting Rings.

One half of mould showing casts in position.
The diagram shows how the mould is fitted together.
The projecting taper rod is of steatite or fireclay, and forms the core
for the three rings.

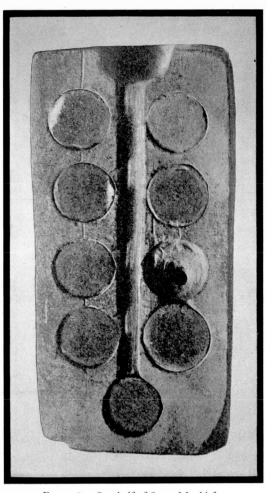

FIG. 238.—One half of Stone Mould for
Coins or Medallions.

From the Museum at Cairo.

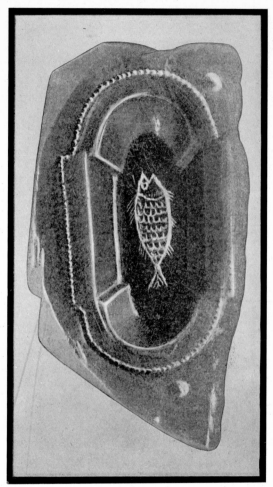

FIG. 239.—Stone Mould for Casting Dishes.

From the Museum at Cairo.

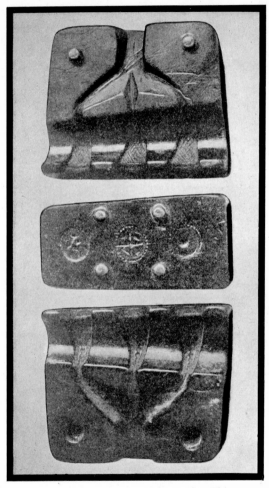

FIG. 240.—Steatite Mould for Casting Rings.

Showing the inside views of the base and the two halves.

tion and realism which frequently defeat their object, the Oriental cares little. Not indeed that he is incapable of it— he can, when necessary, do work of the utmost refinement of surface—but he aims at other things.

The next illustration, fig. 251, shows the maker of cast vessels preparing, by a method very similar to that indicated by Theophilus, the cores of the vases and bowls, a group of which is seen in the background.

The core, as Theophilus describes it, is turned in a mixture of clay, then dried, and the thickness of the vase added in wax or tallow. The Indian method differs from this slightly, in that the clay model of the vase is itself turned down in the lathe until a thickness equal to that of the future vase has been removed. The photograph and the diagrams, figs. 252, 253, will make this point quite clear.

This difference simplifies the process very greatly. The Hindoo artist turns the actual shape of the vase in a mixture of chopped straw and clay. Then when the model is dry, moulds in the same clay the outer mould upon the model itself, using powdered charcoal to separate the two. When the outer mould, which is made in two halves, is dry and complete, the inner mould is reduced in size on the lathe to the exact thickness of the metal. The mould is then complete. Fig. 252

FIG. 252.

shows a mould broken in half to enable the arrangement to be seen clearly.

Fig. 254 shows the Benares brass-workers engaged on the enrichment of large beaten vessels.

410

The interior of the bowl is covered with a layer of pitch about 1½ inches thick.

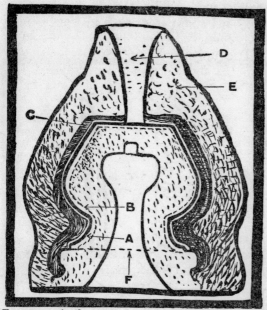

FIG. 253.—A, the original outline of the core and the true outline of the vase when cast; B, the dotted line shows the amount turned from the core after the outer mould has been made round it; C, the inner casing of fine stuff charcoal and fine clay; D is the pour; E, section through the outer mould; F, the register moulding which takes the bearing of the outer portion of the mould.

When cold the vessel is supported on a stout board or block of wood out of which

a hollow fitting the curve of the vessel
has been excavated. This keeps the work
steady and enables the worker to turn
the bowl about from time to time as may
be necessary.

The only tools are a few chisels and
punches and a hammer and pincers. As

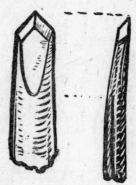

FIG. 256.

will be seen, the design is in every case
most beautifully adapted to the surface
to be decorated. Every curve has its own
significance, and every pattern its message.

The work of the engraver shown in
fig. 255 is particularly interesting because
the method and the tools are very like
those described in the chapters on Japanese
inlaid work. The gravers, instead of

412

being simple lengths of steel, are mounted in long hard-wood handles, and look like small carpenters' chisels. Instead of a hammer a piece of hard, heavy wood about 12 inches long and 1¼ inches square is used as a mallet.

The shape of the cutting end of one of these tools is shown in fig. 256.

The work is simply supported on a low three-legged stool having one leg shorter than the other two so that the work is inclined towards the worker. The tool is held in exactly the way described for the Japanese outlining tool, and the pattern, when complete, is filled with a composition of shellac and powdered colours melted and driven into the cuts with a piece of iron shaped like a soldering-bit.

The superfluous colour is cleaned off with a rag soaked in spirits of wine or petrol.

The sight of these accomplished artists working continually for what here would be thought a derisory fee, gaining happiness and spiritual growth from their tasks ; beautifying simply, easily, naturally, things required for daily use by their countrymen, fills one with a kind of hunger for a like happy activity. It makes one long for an activity rooted in and nurtured

by a common need and rewarded beyond
the daily fee by general interest in and
love for the labour of the hand.

And the hope arises that the young
workers in the West may come to realise
that happiness and handiwork are inseparable companions ; that craft is more
desirable than riches, faculty more than
honour, and that skill can only come
through the breath that is divine.

CHAPTER XLVIII

On Design.

As this book is used by teachers as well as students,
this chapter, the compressed result of many musings,
has been added as a statement of one of the myriad
ways in which the complex question of design may be
considered.

On Design DESIGN and workmanship are indivisible.
The thing made may reveal more of one
than the other. Idea may exceed skill or
fall below it. In any work worthy of
the name, there must be a balance
of both. Not equilibrium but balance.
In all great work, the mysterious, in-
calculable, arresting element of idea, the
underlying conception, holds, and must
ever hold, first place.

Design and workmanship are inseparable,

414

because the form of the work is the more
or less conscious expression of the intimate
spiritual structure of the mind of the
worker. The plan of his work is, in some
sort, the plan of his soul. One may
imagine that, just as each known element,
though merging into others by imper-
ceptible gradations, is in its typical form
characterised by atoms having a definite
molecular structure and inter-relation, so
each mind has, as it were, an individual
molecular structure, traceable in all its
manifestations, separating it from and yet
binding it up with universal mind. Design is, in fact, a function of vitality. It
is admirable in proportion to the amount
and intensity of that vitality.

When we say that a design is original,
we mean that more than usual of the
worker's life has escaped into the work.
Originality is no rarity. Everybody is
original. Everybody can design, if not
supremely, at least beautifully. There
are no dull pupils ; only undeveloped
teachers. No unskilled workers ; only
spirits half-awake. What we call a man's
limitations are the facets of his soul.
Set him in his true place, and by their
virtue he will shine and transcend them.

To produce designers it is, however, necessary that each worker should be encouraged or induced to have confidence in, and give free play to, that creative thought by which his body was made and is sustained; to realise that what he seeks without, awaits within. The shaping power, implicit, inherent in all things, comes when called and not before.

Nothing exists which is not, in some sort, the embodiment of design, because nothing exists which is not an outcome of memory. The sense of beauty is memory. Love is memory. As Butler says, " Memory is an ultimate and original power, the source and unifying bond of our whole conscious life."[1] Matter itself is a phase of memory, a whirl of thought in the world of ether; thought ceaselessly reshaping itself, seeking to enlarge upon the archetype, extend the bounds of the world-foundation, add new universes to its dominion. Design, in this aspect, is formalised memory; habit expressed in form; the thought-habit, to which each type of organised matter owes its shape. Rock and flood and star, all forms with

[1] S. Butler, " Unconscious Memory." Published by A. Fifield.

416

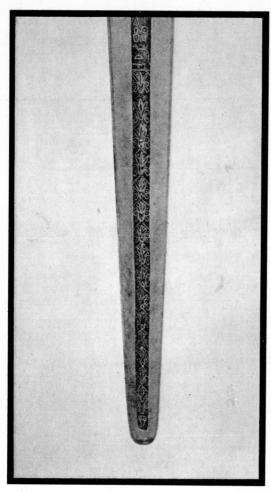

FIG. 236A.—Blade of Egyptian Inlaid Dagger.

From the Museum at Cairo.

See also page 401.

FIG. 248.—Lota Maker's Lathe, Moulds, and Turning Tools.
Photograph, by courtesy of the Management of the Coronation Exhibition.
See page 406.

417

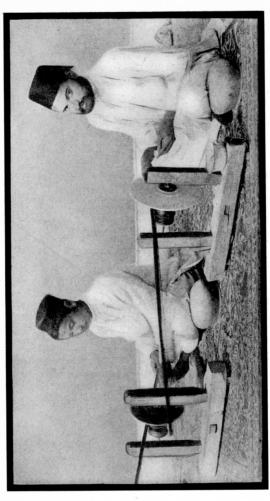

FIG. 249.—Indian Stone-cutting and Polishing Lathes.
Photograph, by courtesy of the Management of the Coronation Exhibition.

See page 407.

FIG. 250.—Sinhalese Repoussé Worker.

Photograph, by courtesy of the Management of the Coronation Exhibition

See page 408.

417

FIG. 251.—Indian Turning Lathe with Kit of Tools and Bow.

Photograph, by courtesy of the Management of the Coronation Exhibition.

See page 409.

FIG. 254.—Benares Brass Chasers at Work.

Photograph, by courtesy of the Management of the Coronation Exhibition.

See page 410.

FIG. 255.—Indian Engraver at Work.

Photograph, by courtesy of the Management of the Coronation Exhibition.

See page 412.

417

which we are familiar, are made by its
agency. Child and flower, field and fruit,
the peak with its cloud, what are they
but the effects of successive recollections,
resurgings of being; transient images of
long world-cycles.

Looked at more inwardly, the thought
suggests itself that form is produced by
the impact of our own and other con-
sciousness. Form changes with perceptive
power. To super-consciousness the re-
florescence of a starry cluster may be what
the birth of the primrose is to us. It may
be that to infra-consciousness the same
flower is built of starry skies and countless
universes whose eternity is our brief
spring. Universes endlessly reborn in
forms which resemble each other because
they are the outcome of the same living
memory. "The flower we see to-day is
the last link of an inconceivably long series
of an organism, which comes down in a
direct line of descent." [1] The perfection
of it is so appealing because we are dimly
conscious of the vast efforts required to
produce such loveliness. We see it rooted,
not in inches of loam, but in æons of toil.

[1] Prof. Hering, " Unconscious Memory," translated
by Samuel Butler.

In its beauty there is something of all the springs of all time. Not one flower presents itself to us, but an eternity of them. Heaven bursting through the skin of earth. At each birth a little lovelier, more captivating than before. In such wise is it with art. It is not of one generation only. Its gestation is secular. Living work, vital design, is recapitulation, the expression of an oft-recurrent memory; the resounding of an oft-repeated phrase in the cosmic symphony. This last word suggests an illustrative parallel.

Who, seeing for the first time some famous singer, has not said : " Can that be she, that wayward-looking, almost inconspicuous being ? " Yet, when she sang, we understood. Her face changed. The whole being seemed extended as by some pythonic influx; transfigured and made radiant through the divine afflatus. The streams of melody flowed out from everywhere at once, throbbing above, beneath, around us. Not the singer but the very principle of song was singing. Not our ears but our throats and hearts heard. Every plexus of nerves was thrilled.

418

She was, at the same time, voice and song; at once the creative and created emotion, the bond that knit to-day, the song-worlds of centuries and spheral harmonies together. In the lullaby, the soul of motherhood found its voice; in the lament, all wifehood. When she sang of love, we heard Psyche herself sobbing softly in the darkness as she pressed through the brake and bramble in the search for Eros. The voice seemed the gate of a world, a gate to which crowded all the memories, passions, and experiences of unnumbered lives, re-awakened by the impulse of song; all now athirst for a moment of new life and new expression.

The child- and the mother- and the lover-notes found each their resurrection, and our life was extended by millenniums.

The singer was not a person only, but the ghost of an ancestral age. That note of passion was not of this birth; it echoed and revivified the far-off ecstasy of a life long since forgotten. It came of a passion not dead, but sleeping beneath the dust of centuries, ready to flame at the lightest breath of spirit. That cry of anguish was not learnt in this life; it sounds again a note of primal pain. The burst of wild entreaty that so moved us was born deep down in time upon the margin of a tropic sea, where in the green forest darkness, love and fierce desire fought the battle of the spirit together.

The mood, the measure, and the music were woven of strands stretching back to the source of life, and the moment of utterance was a cross section of being. In the gradations of a tone, the soul ran through the memories of ages. The muted murmurings of young emotion and the full chords of passion found completion and roundness in the spiritual and material structure they helped to build. For the body was built by pain and love, twin strands of memory.

The song was an epitome of life ; the life that enters with a cry, and with a sigh departs. The singer was a charged imprint of world-memory. Her activities, though seeming individual, were collective ; her voice, though crystal clear, the cry of clustered millions. A being in appearance, separate and detached, yet in truth forming one vast organism with all its ancestry ; an organism of which none can tell the past, divine the plan, or forecast the future, for it changes as it grows, and with each acqui-

sition opens out new spiritual territory
and evolves new powers. Close-knit with
every other organism, its existence implicit
in theirs as they in it, each is not a part
merely but is the universe. As with
individuals, so with races. Civilisations
flower and fruit and fade, each growing
from the débris of those which went
before, each expressing in some sort the
activities of a life so vast as to be scarce
conceivable ; a group-life of whose form
nothing yet is known, though each
civilisation is bound up with all its
predecessors, for their features grow
fainter as they recede into "the dark
backward and abysm" of thought, and
shape and plan escape us.

Knowledge is the store of cosmic experience, and to be wise is to have access
to that store and to add to it by use.
Art is the creative manifestation of
Knowledge.

What is true of song is true of other
arts. The worker is a gate of memory, a
reservoir of cosmic energy ; world-life, seeking new births in new yet familiar forms.
The strand of life-hunger, on which his
myriad existences are strung, stretches out
into the infinite like a vine tendril blindly

feeling after new supports for the coming oft-repeated harvest.

The work is the précis and sum of past and the promise and symbol of future experience. Most original when most nearly derived, most expressive when most reticent ; the more intimately human, the more obviously divine. Yet, withal, the highest conceivable perfection of work is a scarce perceptible step towards that which will be.

The only limits of power are the bounds of belief. Whom the past impels and the future calls, will travel far and swiftly. None need be discouraged. If the worker seek the craft only, perfect himself in that, supple body, subdue mind, and harness spirit to the daily task, he cannot fail of enlightenment. " Live the life, and you shall know the doctrine," said the wise one.

Chuang Tzu conveys the age-old lesson in another way.

"Ch'ing, the chief carpenter, was carving wood into a stand for hanging musical instruments. When finished, the work appeared to those who saw it as though of supernatural execution.

" And the Prince of Lu asked him, say-

ing, 'What mystery is there in your
art?'

" ' No mystery, your Highness,' replied
Ch'ing, 'and yet there is something. When
I am about to make such a stand I guard
against any diminution of my vital power.
I first reduce my mind to absolute
quiescence. Three days in this condition,
and I become oblivious of any reward to
be gained. Five days and I become
oblivious of any fame to be acquired.
Seven days and I become unconscious of
my four limbs and my physical frame.

" ' Then, with no thought of the Court
present to my mind, my skill becomes
concentrated, and all disturbing elements
from without are gone. I enter some
mountain forest. I search for a suitable
tree. It contains the form required;
which is afterwards elaborated. I see the
stand in my mind's eye, and then set to
work. Otherwise there is nothing. I
bring my own natural capacity into relation with that of the wood. What was
suspected to be of supernatural execution
in my work was due solely to this.' " [1]

These words, written three or four

[1] From Chuang Tzu, translated by H. Giles.
Published by Quaritch.

centuries before our era, are still alive with vital truth. No work has such survival power as that done under like conditions. For myself this little tale enshrines not only a religion and a philosophy but also the root and flower and fruit of Design.

PLATES

PLATE I.—Shows a Group of Personal
Jewellery from South Kensington Museum.
The first three specimens on the plate are
ear-rings of Roman workmanship, but obviously made under the influence of Greek
or Etruscan traditions. The first shows
the use of filagree and twisted wire and
simple methods of using rough-cut precious
stones. The second shows a pierced setting for a pearl attached to a rough piece
of emerald. The third a similar pierced
setting applied to a bit of emerald crystal
roughly polished. The gold is fine gold,
and the workmanship of the whole exceedingly simple, yet exceedingly effective.
The fourth Object is a piece of late Spanish
work, but it shows a beautiful way of
using seed pearls, and as a piece of craftsmanship is very near akin to the first three.

427

The vine leaves are scorpered out of thick sheet silver, and gilt and enamelled. The hand is also enamelled.

PLATE II.—*Anglo-Saxon Brooches from the British Museum.* No. 1. *Gold Brooch found at Abingdon;* 2 and 3. *Silver Brooches found at Faversham.* These brooches are magnificent examples of the value of repetition and rhythm in design. The attention of the student is particularly directed in the case of the Abingdon plate to the rich colour of the original, to the sumptuousness of the design which is yet almost rudimentary in its simplicity, and to the extreme ingenuity of the craftsmanship by which the thin coils of compound wire are twisted into almost realistic presentments of serpents.

The Ring of Ethelwulf is a good example of the common-sense design. The craftsman has taken all the space he could on the top of the finger, but where a broad ring would prevent the finger from bending he has narrowed it down to a simple band.

PLATE III.—No. 1. *Gold Belt Buckle found at Taplow.* A very fine example of the use of corded wire as a contrast to cloison inlay.

428

No 2. *A Gold Brooch found at Dover*,
showing the richness produced by concentric rings of tiny scrolls enclosed by plain
and twisted wires. This surface affords
an ideal foil for the red garnet inlay.

PLATE IV.—The Necklace is of Anglo-Saxon workmanship, found at Desborough,
Northamptonshire. It is given as an example of the use of uncut stones, and the
fine effect produced by simple coiled wire.
The small brooches are fourteenth-century
inscribed brooches of English workmanship given to show the beauty of severe
and simple forms.

PLATE V.—*The Shrine of the Bell of
Conall Cael.* This shrine of bronze and
silver and precious stones gives an admirable illustration of several of the methods
described by Theophilus in his book of
" Divers Arts." The beautiful little panels
of scroll work were impressed in stamps
carved out of iron or bronze, and the
figures are in cast bronze. It would be
difficult to find a more romantic or more
suggestive design. The crystal sphere on
which the crucifix rests makes the whole
work look quite magical.

PLATE VI.—*The Gold Cup of the Kings
France and England.* Perhaps the most

429

beautiful piece of gold work in the world.
The photograph, good as it is, can, however, convey no suggestion of the wonder-
ful colour and splendour of the original. It
is given to show that all work to be decorated by enamel should be simple in form.

PLATE VII.—No 1. *An English Gold
Brooch, fourteenth century*, set with pearls,
cabochon sapphires, and emeralds. An example showing shaped settings for pearls,
claw settings for the stones, and carved
and pierced dragon bosses as a contrast to
the stones. A model of built-up design.

No. 2. *A Roman Ring of Gold*, coiled up
out of thin wire and soldered into a solid
band. An example of the beauty of absolutely simple craftsmanship.

No. 3. *A Russian Pendant*, illustrating
the value of filagree surfaces as a contrast
to the watery sheen of precious stones.

No. 4. *A Gold Ring, Roman*, an example
of pierced and carved work.

No. 5. *A Gold Ring*, built up of strands
of thin metal united by a repoussé boss as
ornament.

PLATE VIII.—*French Brooches of the
13th and 14th centuries*. The first built up
out of thin sheet metal, the second carved
out of the solid. The first is an example

of the use of leaves made as described in the chapter on Rings. The settings are simple cones of thin sheet metal wrapped round the stones. At the back of the brooch is a beautiful border in niello. Every student should see this brooch and study it for himself.

PLATE IX.—*A Processional Cross, fifteenth century, German workmanship.* This cross is, as it were, a resumé of the whole goldsmith's art. There is hardly a process which has not been used in its manufacture. Twisted wire of every degree of complexity, stamped work, carved work, beaten work, cast work, and enamelling—all unite to make a most beautiful whole. As a study of compression in design it could hardly be surpassed.

PLATE X.—*A French thirteenth-century Chalice.* This illustrates the decoration of chalices by impressed work described by Theophilus.

PLATE XI.—*Ciborium in copper gilt,* set with jewels and panels of enamel. A splendid example of the value of clearly defined spaces, and the beauty which may result from the arrangement of rigid shapes within such spaces. Italian, fourteenth century.

431

PLATE XII.—*Pastoral Staff in copper gilt*,
set with enamel. Given as an example of
the right use of enamel. Italian, fourteenth century.

PLATE XIII.—*Norwegian Bridal Crown
in silver gilt.* This shows the possibilities
of work in thin sheet metal.

PLATE XIV.—*The Alfred Jewel.* An
example of the decorative value of in-
scriptions, of the use of coiled and beaded
wire, and the right use of enamels.

PLATE XV.—*Pendants, Brooches, and a
Ring by the author.* In gold and jewels
and enamels.

PLATE XVI.—No. 1. *A Necklace in opals,
emeralds, and pearls by the author.* Most
of the stones in the necklace were cut
and polished by the method described in
chapter xxx.

No. 2. *A Shrine Ring*, enclosing an image
of the Holy Mother and Child.

432

PLATE I.—1, 2, 3, Roman Earrings; 4, Sixteenth-century
Spanish Pendant, in Silver Gilt, Enamel, and Pearls.

(South Kensington Museum.)

PLATE II.—1, Anglo-Saxon Brooch, found near Abingdon; 2, 3, Anglo-Saxon Brooches, found near Faversham; 4, Anglo-Saxon Ring, found at Laverstock.

(British Museum.)

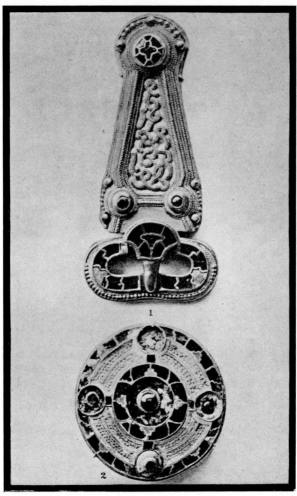

PLATE III.—1, Anglo-Saxon Belt Buckle, found at
Taplow; 2, Anglo-Saxon Brooch, found at Dover.
(British Museum.)

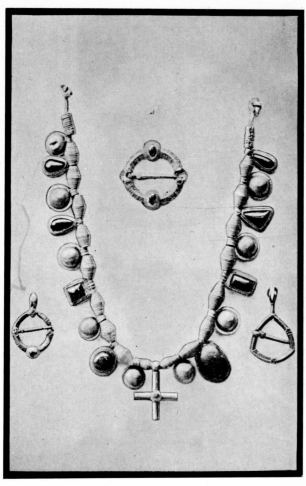

PLATE IV.—Anglo-Saxon Necklace and Fourteenth-century English Inscribed Brooches.

(British Museum.)

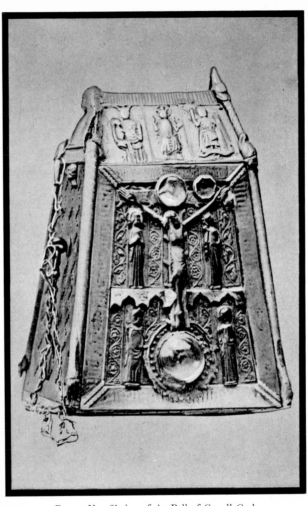

PLATE V.—Shrine of the Bell of Conall Cael.
(British Museum.)

PLATE VI.—Gold Cup of the Kings of France and England.
(British Museum.)

PLATE VII.—1, English Gold Brooch, Fourteenth century;
2, 3, 5, Roman Gold Rings; 4, Russian Pendant.

(British Museum.)

PLATE VIII.—1, French Gold Brooch, Thirteenth century;
2, French Gold Brooch, Fourteenth century.

(South Kensington Museum.)

PLATE IX.—Processional Cross.
(Villingen.)

PLATE X.—French Chalice, Thirteenth century.
(South Kensington Museum.)

PLATE XI.—Ciborium, in Copper-gilt.
(South Kensington Museum.)

PLATE XII.—Pastoral Staff, Italian.
(South Kensington Museum.)

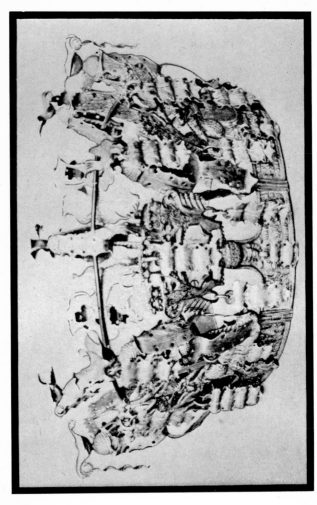

PLATE XIII.—Norwegian Bridal Crown.

(South Kensington Museum.)

PLATE XIV.—Front View of Alfred Jewel.
(Ashmolean Museum.)

PLATE XV.—1, Belt Buckle, in Pale Gold, with Enamel,
Rubies, Sapphires, and Pearls; 2, Pendant, in Pale
Gold, with Beryl and Sapphire; 3, Gold Ring, set with
Rubies, Emeralds, and Pearls.

(By the Author.)

PLATE XVI.—1, Necklace, in Gold, set with Emeralds, Opals, Sapphires, and Pearls; 2, Front View of the Lid of a Shrine Ring. The Lid is hinged and forms a Cover to an Enamelled Panel of the Holy Mother and Child.

(By the Author.)

THE following sections of mediæval cups and chalices, taken from Nightingale's "Church Plate of Wiltshire" (published by Messrs. Bennet Brothers, Salisbury), are given as suggestions of form. The section to the right of Plate I. is that of the Foundress' cup given in the Frontispiece. The student is referred to "Old Cambridge Plate" (published by the Cambridge Antiquarian Society) for further beautiful examples of silverwork.

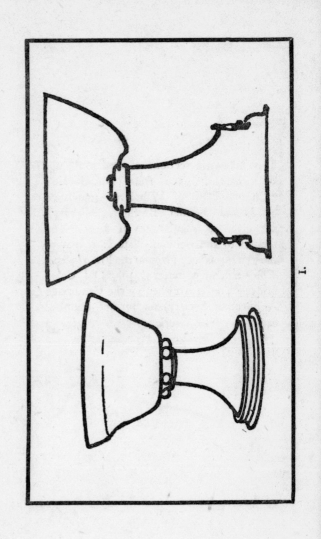

I.

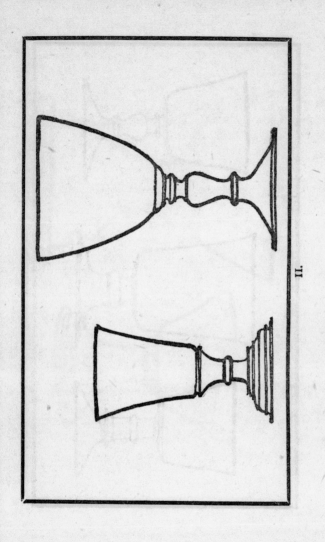

II.

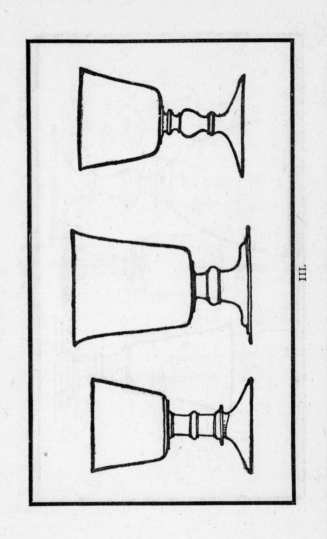

III.

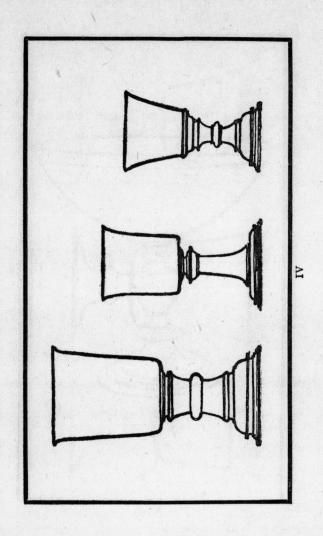

IV

V.

PRACTICAL
RECIPES

Contact Gilding.—Take of yellow prussiate of potash,
2 oz.; carbonate of potash, 1 oz.; common
salt, 1½ oz.; water, 1 quart. Boil the water in
an enamelled saucepan. When boiling add the
salts one by one. Stir well with a glass rod, and
continue boiling for two or three minutes, after
which add slowly a solution of 2 dwts. of
chloride of gold dissolved in a little water, stirring
the mixture the while. Allow it to cool and
preserve it in a stoppered bottle. When required
for gilding take a little of the liquid and heat it
nearly to boiling point, then place the article,
thoroughly cleansed, on a piece of bright, clean
zinc, and immerse it in the solution, when it will,
after a few moments, be covered with a film of
gold. (From "The Jeweller's Assistant in
Working in Gold," by G. Gee.)

Greek Gilding for Copper, Gilding Metal or Bronze.—
Dissolve equal parts of sal-ammoniac and cor-
rosive sublimate in strong nitric acid. With the
mixture make a solution of fine gold and con-
centrate the solution by evaporation. When you
think it sufficiently concentrated dip the object to
be gilded after it has been pickled clean, or paint
it on with a brush. The solution will blacken it

471

instantly if it be strong enough. This done, heat the object to redness, when the gold will appear.

Grecian Gilding, another way.—Take equal parts bichloride of mercury and chloride of ammonia, dissolve in nitric acid, add small portion of gold chloride, and dilute with water. To gild silver articles, brush the composition over them, and expose them to just enough heat to volatilise the mercury. This done the work can be burnished. (From "The Jeweller's Assistant in Working in Gold," by G. Gee.)

Fire-Gilding for Steel, Iron, or Copper.—Scrape the copper or iron with the scraper and burnisher, warm the object, if it be steel or iron, until it takes a bluish tinge; if it be copper, to a corresponding heat. You will now apply the first layer of gold leaf and burnish it on lightly. The work must next be exposed to a gentle heat and another layer applied. If you wish to make the coating of gold extra strong, use two leaves of gold at each operation. The work must not be finally burnished bright until the last leaf of gold has been laid on and the work is cold.

Cement for Engravers.—Melt best pitch in an iron vessel, and when completely liquid stir in yellow ochre or red ochre in fine powder in a sufficient quantity to colour the mixture. Pour it out on a smooth oiled stone or marble slab.

To Polish Enamel.—After rubbing it down with the corundum file take a small rod of tin or pewter, and after anointing it with fine tripoli or rottenstone, grind the surface of the enamel evenly with this. Next take a stick of lime wood and use that with rotten-stone in the same way, and finish with putty powder and a buff stick.

Good Solder for Gold.—Fine silver, 1 part; fine copper, 1 part; fine gold, 2 parts. Melt the copper and silver together, and when well mixed add the gold.

To Unsolder a Piece of Work.—Paint those joints which are not to be unsoldered with a mixture of loam and water to which a little common salt has been added. This will protect them. When dry scrape the portions next to the part to be unsoldered and paint it all well with borax. Then just give enough heat to melt the solder, and remove the part with the pincers. Or if this be impossible owing to the nature of the work, before unsoldering fix a stout iron wire to the part to be removed and lift it off in that way.

For Japanese, Persian, Indian, and Egyptian recipes see page 283 and onwards.

473

GLOSSARY

Alloy, base metal added to silver or gold to give hardness or colour. Also, any combination of different metals by fusion.

Alloy bronze. See *Bronze alloy*.

Annealing, softening metal by making it red-hot and cooling slowly.

Backing, the coating of enamel on the back surface of enamelled plaques. Also, the washings and wastings of ground enamel used to coat the backs of enamel plaques.

Back-saw, a saw made of a thin ribbon of steel, such as a clock-spring, fixed in a brass back, used for dividing metal.

Basse taille, low cut carving in metal beneath the level of the surface, used in enamelling. The drawing or modelling of the subject is given by the different depths of cutting. The enamel naturally appears darker over the deeper cuttings and *vice versa*.

Beck-iron, a T-shaped anvil or stake used in hammer work. The arms of the T are long—one is round, slender, and tapering ; the other has a flat upper surface.

Bezel, the thin slip of metal inside the shutting edge of a box or casket.

475

Board sweep, the filings of precious metal swept from the work-board, and kept for refining.

Bossing up, beating out sheet metal from the back into rough approximations of the form required.

Broche, a tapering prism of steel with sharp edges, used for enlarging holes and the insides of tubes.

Bronze alloy (Japanese)

Copper	.	.	.	75 % to 80	} 8 lbs.
Lead	.	.	.	25 % to 28	
Shirome	.	.	.	3 ozs.	

Burnishers, handled tools with points, knobs, or flattened surfaces of hardened steel, agate, blood-stone, or hæmatite, highly polished, used for polishing the surface of metal by compression.

Burr, the raised and roughened edge of a cutting or incision made in a sheet of metal by a chisel or cutting tool.

Cabochon, a method of cutting precious stones without facets. The surface of the rough stone is ground away until it is evenly rounded and smooth to the touch. The back is then ground flat, or, in the case of carbuncles, concave. Stones cut in this way are also called " tallow drop " stones. There is also the double cabochon which is naturally like two simple cabochons put back to back.

Casting-sand, a natural or artificial mixture of fine loam and sand, used to make moulds for casting.

Cement stick, a short taper handle of wood, the upper end notched and covered with cement, made of pitch or resin and powdered brick-dust, used to hold small objects while being engraved.

Champlevé, a process of enamelling on metal in which the ground of the pattern is cut away with scorpers into a series of shallow troughs into which the enamel is melted, the surface being afterwards ground smooth and polished.

Chasing, surface modelling of metal with hammer
and punches.

Chaton, the central ornament of a ring.

Chenier, metal tubes used in making hinges.

Chuck, a moveable vice with three or more adjustable
jaws meeting in the centre used as a turning lathe.

Cire perdue, the waste-wax process of casting direct
from the original wax model. The model having
been enclosed in sand rammed closely round it, is
melted away and its place taken by molten metal.

Cloison, an enclosing ribbon of wire, which, being
soldered edgewise on a metal ground, makes a
trough into which enamel is melted.

Collar, a ring made of several layers of stout leather,
sewn or riveted together, used to support the
pitch bowl.

Core, the heart of a mould for casting hollow objects.

Corn tongs, small tweezers, used for picking up stones,
bits of solder, &c., and adjusting them.

Cramps, bits of thick iron wire bent to various shapes,
used to hold work together while being soldered.

Crown setting, an open setting with rebated points to
hold the stone.

Crucible, a vessel of fireclay or other refractory
material, used for melting metal, so called because
they were formerly stamped with the sign of the
Cross.

Cupel, a block of compressed bone ash with a cup-
shaped depression, used in a muffle for purifying
gold and silver. The precious metal is wrapped
up in seven or eight times its weight of lead, and
when melted the lead runs away into the bone
ash, carrying the impurities with it.

Damascene, the art of incrusting metals with other
usually more precious metals, once practised
mainly in Damascus.

477

Doming-block, a cube of metal with hemispherical depressions of various sizes in the sides, used with doming punches for making hollow balls out of sheet metal.

Doming punches, punches with globular heads, made in sets to fit the hollows of the doming-block. They may be in steel, brass, or boxwood.

Draw-bench, a low bench with a winch at one end, which, acting on a board strap attached by a strong iron loop to a pair of pincers called draw-tongs, is used to draw wire through the draw-plate held against stops fixed at the other end of the bench.

Draw-plate, a flat plate of steel pierced with a row or rows of graduated holes, and used for drawing wire.

Face-plate, a square of thick steel plate with the surface ground perfectly level, used when filing to test the truth of the work.

Facing, the operation of giving a smooth surface to a casting mould by dusting on a finer material. The facings most generally used are powdered charcoal, flour and charcoal, French chalk, soot, and pea-flour.

False core, the removable section of a casting mould arranged to draw out clearly from a piece of undercut work.

Flask, an iron frame used to contain the sand while being rammed round an object to be cast.

Flatting stone, a flat stone used for rubbing down the edges of boxes and cups to a level.

Flaunching, filing a chamfer on the edge or side of any object.

478

Flinking, the process of stabbing with a sharp pointed graver the surface of metal which is to be enamelled. Its object is to give a key to the film of glass, and prevent it from flaking away from the metal.

Flux, any material used to protect the surface of metal from oxidation when exposed to heat, or to aid in the liquefaction or purification of metals when necessary to melt them. These are powdered charcoal, borax-glass, borax, saltpetre, carbonate of soda, sal-ammoniac, powdered glass, common salt, and sulphur.

Gallery, a setting with perforated sides for a stone or a panel of enamel.

Gate or *get*, the hole or channel arranged in a casting mould for the access of the metal.

Girdle, that edge of a precious stone which is fixed in the setting.

Graining tool, a hollow-headed punch with a wooden handle, used for rounding the heads of pins used in fixing parts of work together.

Graver, a kind of scorper or small chisel for cutting lines on the surface of metal.

Hare's foot, the dried foot of a hare, used as a brush to dust away gold and silver filings from the board.

Hesri Tagane, a name of a Japanese matting tool.

Hira-Zogwan, inlaying of an object with different metals.

Ingot, a block of metal, generally rectangular, cast into a convenient shape for rolling, or wire-drawing, or remelting.

Joint file, a flat strip of steel with rounded edges on which are file cuts. It is used for making grooves for hinges.

479

Joint tool, a flat plate of steel fixed in a handle and pierced with a triangular hole. The point of the triangle is towards the handle, and in the base in the thickness of the metal is a thumbscrew. The ends of a tube when secured at the apex of the triangle by the screw can be filed quite true.

Justifier, a scorper with two cutting edges at right angles, used in cutting bearings for the stones.

Kami tsuchi, paper clay made of fine casting sand, Japanese paper, and ordinary potters' clay.

Katakiribori, engraving and reproducing the movement of brushwork.

Kiri tagane, a small, sharp cutting chisel used in Japanese inlaid work.

Knop, any bulbous projection on a shaft or pillar of a cup or candlestick, &c.

Knurling tool, a small steel wheel with a concave edge pitted with tiny hollows. When fitted in a slotted steel handle and run backwards and forwards along a wire soldered on a plate it produces a row of beads.

Lemel (French " Limaille," filings), the filings and scrap of precious metal collected in the skin of the work bench. It is carefully preserved and, when enough has been collected, is melted and the metal refined for subsequent use.

Loam, a fatty, ochreous earth used in casting.

Luting, the application of a mixture of loam and water, fire-clay and water, whitening or tripoli, or rouge and water to protect parts of metal while other parts are soldered.

Mandrel, a rod of metal or any section, used either for tube-drawing or for coiling wire in the making of chains. Also, the tapered rod of steel used in making rings.

480

Matrix, the mother-form or mould for cast work.

Matt tool, a repoussé punch with a flat, granulated end, used for making a grained surface on metal.

Mop, a tangled boss of fine binding-wire fixed on a wire handle and used to support small articles while being soldered with the mouth blow-pipe. Also, a contrivance for polishing made of a number of discs of calico fixed to a wooden spindle. When put on the polishing lathe, it becomes rigid by rapid revolution. The edges are then smeared with rouge and the object to be polished pressed against it.

Namekuri tagane, an outlining chisel with a rounded bevel used in Japanese inlaid work.

Narashi tagane, the name of a Japanese matting tool used in inlaid work.

Niello from *nigello*, a black very fasibile alloy of sulphur, lead, silver and copper used in decorating engraved work on silver or gold.

Odd side, the temporary half of a casting mould arranged to support the model while the false cores are being made over it.

Paillon, a snippet of solder.

Patina, an artificially produced oxide for the decoration of bronzes and other metal work.

Panel, a snippet of solder.

Parting sand, powdered brick-dust or bathbrick, used to sprinkle on the face of a mould.

Pearl-tool, a punch and a circular concavity on the top used in chasing.

Perloir, a chasing punch with a concave tip, used for making convex beads on the surface of metal.

Pickle, solutions of various acids in water, used for removing the films of oxide and sulphides from the surface of metal. The acids used are nitric acid, hydrochloric acid, and sulphuric acid, and a very ordinary mixture is half acid and half water. This solution is as strong as necessary for general use.

Piece-mould, a mould for casting undercut work, made in removable sections, called false cores, so arranged that, when the mould is complete, it can be taken to pieces, the model removed, and the mould re-formed for casting.

Pin, the wedge of hard wood, generally beech, fixed in the bow of the jeweller's bench, used to hold work up against the file.

Pitch-block, a block of wood covered with pitch, used as a support for metal in repoussé work or chasing.

Planishing, giving a plane or level surface to a sheet of metal by the use of a broad, smooth-faced hammer and an anvil. Also, giving a smooth face to a beater's cup or other object in sheet metal by the same means.

Plaque, a plate of metal slightly domed and prepared for enamelling. Also, the same plate when coated with enamel.

Plique à jour, transparent enamel which, being without metal backing, gets its strength from variously folded ribbons of metal within the thickness of the enamel, in the same way that a stained glass window is strengthened.

Pour, the gate or inlet for the metal to run into a mould for casting.

Punches doming. See *Doming punches*.

Repoussé, the method of beating out sheet metal from the back with hammers and punches.

Revolving trammel. See *Trammel, revolving*.

Riffles, files with curved and variously shaped ends, used for filing up the surfaces of castings and for cleaning up any surface for which an ordinary file cannot be used.

482

Riser, a channel scraped out of one surface of a piece-mould to allow the escape of air. Also, in a waste-wax mould the slender rod of wax arranged to make a similar air channel when melted out of the mould.

Router, a graver or small triangular file bent at right angles and ground to a sharp edge, used for cutting the groves in metal for the joints of boxes, &c.

Runners, in piece-moulds, channels for the entry of metal into various parts of the mould. In waste-wax moulds the rod of wax arranged to provide a similar channel when melted out of the mould.

Sand-bag, a flat circular bag of leather filled with sand, used for bossing up metal upon.

Scorpers, small hand chisels of various shapes, used to engrave metal.

Scraper, a tool made from an old file by sharpening the point on a stone to a three-sided pyramid. Used for scraping clean edges and surfaces to be soldered and for cleaning up work generally.

Shakudo. An alloy of copper and gold.

Shiage Tsuchi, finishing clay. A mixture of casting sand made pasty with clay alone.

Shibuichi, an alloy of copper and silver.

Shigata Tsuchi (core clay), made with clay, sand, and chopped straw.

Shirome, a natural alloy chiefly composed of antimony.

Smooth, a fine cut file for finishings.

Snap, a spring-catch for a bracelet or necklace.

Snarling-irons, long Z-shaped levers fixed in a vice and used for bossing out the surface of vessels from the inside. They act by rebounding from the blow of the hammer near the fixed end.

483

Stake, a small anvil. They are of many forms, from the bench stake, a square block of iron faced with steel, to the variously curved bars with rounded, bulbous, or spoon-shaped ends, used when fixed in a vice for beating up cups, &c. A poker fixed upright in the floor makes an excellent stake.

Stones cabochon. See *Cabochon.*

Stones, flatting. See *Flatting stones.*

Stone Washita. See *Washita stone.*

Swage-block, a modified draw-plate, made in removable sections held in a frame by a screw. Used for drawing wire or mouldings. The holes are arranged in the contiguous surfaces of two blocks, and the size of the wire or moulding can be regulated by the screw.

Sweep, the refuse from the floor of the jeweller's workshop which is collected, burnt, and the metallic residue melted and refined for use in the same way as lemel.

Taka-Zogwan, similar to Hira Zogwan but inlaid in relief.

Tama Tsuchi, a grade coarser clay than Kami Tsuchi for casting, made of chopped tow, sand, and wet clay.

Tang, that end of a graver or file which is prepared for insertion into a handle.

Tracer, a chisel-shaped punch used in outlining for repoussé work.

Trammel revolving, a templete fixed to a horizontal arm of wood and capable of being revolved round a fixed centre, used to make circular moulded bases and cores in casting.

Treblet, a taper mandrel or steel on which rings are made.

484

Tsuta Tsuchi, chopped straw clay, coarsest grade of casting clay, made of straw, wet clay, and casting sand.

Ukibori, Japanese term for chasing.

Washita stone, a fine grained American whetstone.

Woodgrain metal, Japanese method of taminating metal akin to that used in producing damascened steel.

Zogwan, Hira. See *Hira Zogwan.*

INDEX

Index

494